# Canadian Studies in Mass Communication

## Asghar Fathi

*Canadian Scholars' Press Inc.*    *Toronto*    *1990*

Canadian Studies in Mass Communication

First published in 1990 by
**Canadian Scholars' Press Inc.,**
**339 Bloor Street West**
**Suite 220**
**Toronto, M5S 1W7**
**Canada**

**Acknowledgements:**

Asghar Fathi, "Problems in Developing Indices of News," from *Journalism Quarterly*, Vol. 50, No. 3. Autumn, 1973. Pages 497-501. Copyright © The Association for Education in Journalism and Mass Communication. 1973. Reprinted by permission. Asghar Fathi, "Diffusion of a 'Happy' News Event," from *Journalism Quarterly*, Vol. 50, No. 2. Summer, 1973. Pages 271-277. Copyright © The Association for Education in Journalism and Mass Communication. 1973. Reprinted by permission. Asghar Fathi, and Carole L. Heath "Group Influence, Mass Media and Musical Taste Among Canadian Students," from *Journalism Quarterly*, Vol. 51, No. 4. Winter, 1974. Pages 705-709. Copyright © The Association for Education in Journalism and Mass Communication. 1974. Reprinted by permission. Asghar Fathi, "Mass Media and a Moslem Immigrant Community in Canada," from *Anthropologica*, Vol. XV, No. 2. Pages 201-230. Copyright © Wilfrid Laurier University Press. 1973. Reprinted by permission.

**Canadian Cataloguing in Publication Data**
Main entry under title:

Canadian Studies in Mass Communication

ISBN 0-921627-47-5

1. Mass Media — Social aspects — Canada.
2. Mass media criticism — Canada.
3. Mass media — Canada — Influence.

P92.C3F38    1990    302.23'0971    C90-095681-X

For David and Jay

# CONTENTS

# PREFACE

This volume consists of seven papers on the sociology of mass communication, three of which (Nos. 1, 2 and 5) have not yet been published, although they have been presented at professional meetings. Except for one co-authored paper (No. 4), they are all the result of over twenty years of research on the various aspects of the Canadian mass communication by myself.

There are two reasons for re-publishing these papers together in one volume. First, as explained in the Introduction, some of these papers have special features. A few are unique in the sociological literature on Canadian mass communication, and fill some gaps in our knowledge of that subject.

Second, those papers which were published in non-Canadian periodicals (Nos. 4, 6 and 7) have seldom come to the attention of Canadian scholars. Re-printing these papers, along with three unpublished studies, under a Canadian title will help to remedy this problem.

# INTRODUCTION

# INTRODUCTION

The seven papers in this volume report on sociological studies of mass communication conducted in Canada during the last twenty years. Some of these papers have special features.

The papers in section two of this volume, the one on the Catholic pulpit in Québec and the other on the pulpit during the American Revolution, deal with the predecessors to the modern mass media and use historical data.

Although valuable historical studies of print as a medium of public communication in Canada, such as the well known volume by Kesterton, are available;[1] historical studies of other long standing public media, such as the pulpit, are rare. It seems that among Canadian historians information about public communication by the church is usually treated as a side issue or building block for another story. The interrelationships between the communicator, channel, audience and effects are seldom the objective of their research.

Among students in the United States, however, there are some who have paid special attention to the role of the pulpit as a medium of public communication in colonial America.[2] In some cases they have even demonstrated the connection between the traditional and modern modes of public communication.[3]

The two papers in section three of this volume deal with the question of how do mass media influence the lives of their audience. As for the relationship between mass media and the ethnic community, ethnic newspapers have received some attention from Canadian students.[4] Non-print media such as radio and television have received less attention.[5] The exposure of ethnic groups to international communication, either via print or electronic media, which is the subject of the first paper in this section, seems to have been largely ignored. With the increase in cross-national and cross-cultural contacts due to the advances of communication technology, however, more research in this area seems necessary.

Regarding the impact of the mass media on the taste of their young audience, including the influence of the recorded music which is the subject of the second paper in section three of this volume, again, we do not find very much research by the sociologists in Canada. If we agree that the examination of the role of the mass media in the socialization of the new generation is important, then with the annual influx of large groups of immigrants to Canada, the investigation of the role of the mass media in the acculturation of the young new Canadians gains an added significance.

Finally, news diffusion studies, which started over forty years ago in United States,[6] have not been attempted in Canada. In this sense the first two papers in section four on the diffusion of sad and happy news events are unique among the sociological studies of mass communication in Canada. Sad and ordinary news events have been studied in the United States extensively,[7] but no diffusion study of a happy news event has yet come to our attention. Thus the

3

paper on the diffusion of the news of Prime Minister Trudeau's secret wedding in 1971 is probably the only one of its kind.

News diffusion studies are important not only because they provide us with an understanding of the audience and the impact of the media. They also give us a picture of the reaction of the different segments of the society to the ongoing events--minor, major, sad or happy. The question of establishing the news value of an event for the various segments of the society is, however, not a simple one. This problem is tackled in the last paper of this volume.

# NOTES

1. See W. H. Kesterton, *History of Journalism in Canada, 1967*.
2. The most recent and probably the most comprehensive report on the role of the pulpit from this particular point of view is Harry S. Stout's, *The New England Soul: Preaching and Religious Culture in Colonial New England, 1986.*
   3. For instance, see David Paul Nord, "The Evangelical Origins of Mass Media in America," *Journalism Monograph*, (88), May, 1984. Several years before my research on the Catholic pulpit in Québec, because of a more visible role of the pulpit in colonial America, I was drawn to the study of the pulpit during the American Revolution. It is my hope that this study would stimulate some studies of the Protestant pulpit as a medium of public communication in a Canadian setting. According to my Canadian students, the parallels between the American and the Canadian Protestant pulpits are legion.
4. See, for instance, W. Turek, The Polish Press in Canada, Toronto, Polish Alliance Press, 1962; "Ethnic Press: The Mixed Medium," in the *Report by Special Committee on Mass Media, Vol. 1, The Uncertain Mirror*, Ottawa, Queen's Printer, pp. 179-183; Jung-Gun Kim, b. Heydenkorn, E. Polyzoi, and M. Boekelman, "The Religious Press in Ethnic Communities," *POLYPHONY* 2, Summer 1978, pp. 37-43; Natural Library of Canada, "The Ethnic Press in Canada: Almost 200 years of Ethnic Journalism," National Library of Canada, June 25, 1980. Ottawa: Supply and Services; and Gerald J. Stortz, "The Irish Catholic Press in Toronto, 1887-1892: The Years of Transition," *Canadian Journal of Communication*, 1984, 10 (3), pp. 27-46; among others.
5. See, for example, Lawrence Lam, "The Role of Ethnic Media for Immigrants: A Case Study of Chinese Immigrants and their Media in Toronto," Canadian Ethnic Studies, Vol XII, No. 1, 1980, pp. 74-92; and Jerome Black and Christian Leithner, "Immigrants and Political Involvement in Canada: The Role of The Ethnic Media," *Canadian Ethnic Studies*, Vol XX, No. 1, 1988, pp. 1-20.
6. The first pioneering study in news diffusion was conducted by D. C. Miller. See his "A Research Note on Mass Communication," *American Sociological Review*, 10, 1945, pp. 691-694.
7. For a report on the state of news diffusion studies see the recent paper by Melvin L. DeFleur, "The Growth and Decline of Research on the Diffusion of the News, 1945-1985," *Communication Research*, Vol. 14, No. 1, 1987, pp. 109-130.

# SECTION I

# PREDECESSORS TO MODERN MEDIA

# THE CATHOLIC PULPIT AS A MEDIUM OF PUBLIC COMMUNICATION IN PRE-CONFEDERATION QUEBEC, CANADA*

*ABSTRACT:* *The significance of the Roman Catholic Church in the development of the French Canadian society has been acknowledged by many scholars. But the involvement of the pulpit as a medium of public communication in the activities of the Church has not yet been singled out for a systematic examination. It is the contention of this paper that an analytical comparison between the Catholic pulpit in pre-Confederation Québec and the modern mass media would show some similarities between the two systems and suggests continuities between modes of public communication through time.*

The significant role of the Roman Catholic Church in the development of French Canadian society has been acknowledged by many scholars. For instance, the Church has been considered instrumental in eliminating the particularism of rural New France and forging a distinct French Canadian culture by establishing links with isolated communities. It is also believed that the Church has preserved a French Canadian identity and the French language through maintaining a link with the past. Again, by involving the parishioners in the development of socio-political issues, especially during British rule, the Church has enabled them to assert themselves, whether in agreement with the Church or not, and surmount many obstacles in their struggle for survival as a distinct society.[1]

However, in spite of the pulpit's direct and prominent involvement as a medium of public communication in these activities of the Roman Catholic Church in Québec, it has, strangely enough, not yet been singled out for examination.

In sociology, this state of affairs is at least partly due to our preoccupation with our own epoch. Thus in the sociological study of mass communication we tend to ignore the types of public communication which in the past have helped sustain empires, assisted in the emergence of values and group cohesion, or facilitated concerted action between various segments of society. We assume that prior to the appearance of newspapers, radio and television, public opinion did not exist, the relationship between a society and its leaders was random and inconsequential, and social movements developed by the appearance of contagious moods.

This paper examines the role of the pulpit of the Roman Catholic Church as a medium of public communication in pre-Confederation Québec. This study is based on the assumption that the operation of a society requires some media of public communication.

Although the structures and functions of traditional pre-industrial and modern industrial societies are not the same, there appear to be some similarities in the functional requirements for both. One of these functional requirements is the existence of public media of communication. Therefore, one can hypothesize that the need for public communication, which in modern societies is satisfied by mass media such as newspapers, radio and television, in pre-modern societies may be satisfied by some other cultural arrangement which is not usually distinct, but rather part of an institution such as religion.

I am not denying that the modern mass media have affected society in significant ways. I am saying rather that public media of communication are not a new phenomenon. By examining the functional alternatives to the modern media in the past, it is possible to discover certain common characteristics of public communication in human society across cultures and time, and thus gain a better understanding of this phenomenon.

*The Catholic Church in New France.* To provide a foundation for our discussion, it is necessary to give a brief description of the situation during the emergence of New France as a colony and its close association with the Roman Catholic Church.

According to Mason Wade, New France was designated by Cardinal Richelieu in 1630 to be a wholly Catholic land, closed to non-Catholics.[2] The colony was founded during the Reformation, when Europe was torn by theological controversies and religious wars. In the new world the French and English colonies continued this antagonism, with the French excluding Protestants from New France and the Puritans barring Catholics from New England. The Counter-Reformation or the Catholic Revival also added to the significance of religious identity in New France with an emphasis on pietism.[3] From the beginning of the settlement in the early seventeenth century, education and the care of the sick and needy were taken over by the Church, whose missionaries also acted as government agents among the Indians.[4] Indeed, some French explorers such as Jacques Cartier believed that they should bring a knowledge of God to the native "savages," and missionaries accompanied the fishing and fur trading boats as early as 1535.[5]

Finally, the strife between Louis XIV of France and Pope Innocent XI in the mid-seventeenth century,[6] accentuated by the rivalry between the politico-military and the ecclesiastical officials in New France,[7] was reflected in the strained relationship between the governors and the bishops. For instance, Bishop Laval, who came to New France in 1659, was able to undermine the positions of a series of Gallican-minded governors and administrators, and for a while effectively develop a theocracy.[8]

## The Catholic Pulpit as a Medium of Public Communication

*The Parish in French Canada.* The first French settlers in New France established themselves along the coasts for convenience in using the waterways. It was not until the early 19th century that inland settlements and dirt roads were built. In order to be as close as possible to one's neighbours, on whom one was dependent for mutual help, the best system for the early settlers was to have a long farm lot with the house on the short side facing the waterfront or the road. When all the land along the waterfront or road was taken, another row of houses was built at a distance from the coast and parallel to it.

This pattern of houses built in long rows or *rangs* inhibited the development of a clustered community or central village, with its general store and craftsmen's shops. While a *rang* had a neighbourhood unity characterized by spontaneous patterns of social interaction, a territorial parish at the beginning was anything but the grouping of a certain number of *rangs*.[9]

Thus the early parishes covered very large areas. These were in effect parish districts, occasionally visited by missionary priests.[10] Later, when the number of priests increased and some areas had their own resident priests, the place where the priest resided became the hub of a real parish, the center for a community of the faithful identified by a specific territory.[11] In this way the parish priest, acting as a catalyst, created the communal parish in Canada.

Often being the only literate person among his parishioners and having contacts with the outside world, in the earlier days in rural areas the priest was not just a spiritual leader. Although removable by the Church authorities, he became the local leader who presided over the *habitants'* social life. While his control over the religious affairs of the parish was restricted by the intervention of the bishop, his temporal leadership in community affairs continually increased. In his weekly sermons during the high mass he was the public informant as well as the mentor of his flock.[12]

Because religious observance intermingled with business and amusement, the parish church became the center of the French Canadian community. Its location also attracted other activities such as stores and craftsmen's shops.[13] Education, welfare and charity being within the domain of the church, these were all established at the parish level. Especially in rural areas, the parish gradually became the local civil and military unit. British rule, beginning in 1759, increased the importance of the parish because of the emphasis on the territorial representative system of government.[14]

The church was frequented by all the people in the district as a place for meeting and for the distribution of information. For most people, and especially for women and children, the weekly Sunday trip to church was their only contact with the outside world. In some areas people even complained that their church was too far for them to attend mass and keep abreast of news.[15]

9

During French rule, regular attendance at mass was required by law. According to police regulations in Québec in 1676, no business was to be conducted on Sundays and the *cabarets* were to be closed in the town during the hours of divine service.[16] In 1710 the *intendant* issued rules for the proper conduct during the mass and specified fines for violators.[17]

The church and its courtyard were also used as a forum and a publicity center. For example, in 1673 four men who had broken into a home in Montréal were sentenced to be exposed at the door of the parish church on a feast day or Sunday following high mass with placards detailing their crime hanging from their necks.[18]

*The Pulpit as a Medium of Public Communication.* However, more important than being a publicity center and a place for the exchange of information and gossip on holidays, it was the role of the Church to be a public communicator via the pulpit. It was through this channel that the Catholic Church exerted most of its influence on the society.

The pulpit was not a channel for religious instruction alone. It was also a channel by which local and other news reached the parishioners.[19] The priests expressed their views on all sorts of events and issues in their sermons. They defined the ethics of everyday life, criticized politicians, and warned people.[20]

The parish priests were required to publish all state decrees. They also had to announce court orders.[21] They read their bishops' *mandements* or pastoral letters from the pulpit. Pastoral letters could be issued for almost any occasion — making announcements, stirring up the population against the enemy in wartime, supporting or condemning government policies, and interpreting events and social issues.[22]

Even in the earlier days, the parishioners were not merely a passive audience; they often gave their communicators feedback. For example, some complained that the Sunday mass was too long; thus in 1691 Bishop Saint-Vallier asked the priests to restrict their sermons to one-half hour. Sometimes during the sermon the audience shuffled their feet and coughed noisily out of annoyance. In later years in the large towns and cities some members of the congregation even left in the middle of the service when they disagreed with the messages from the pulpit.[23] According to Jaenen, the parish priests "spoke out on all manners of questions from their pulpits, but they were unable to coerce the colonists into obedient submission when the latter were unconvinced or opposed."[24]

*The Role of the Pulpit in Church — State Relations.* To demonstrate the place of the pulpit as a medium of public communication in pre-Confederation Québec we begin with three examples of its role in the relationship between the two powers which dominated the society — the Church and the state. Two of these examples come from the time of French rule and one from the British era.

In discussing events during the French era some important points should be kept in mind. First, the Church and the state in New France were not officially two distinct systems. The King of France was also the official head of the Church. For instance, Louis XIV used this power to regulate the role of the pulpit as a publicity channel and to determine the amount of tithe that   parishioners had to pay.[25] However, although the bishop of Québec and the two other principal members of the Sovereign Council — the governor and the *intendant* [26]— were all appointed by the King, each had a separate realm and different interests to protect and promote. Moreover, the French Minister of Marine, who was responsible for the administration of the colony, continuously warned the governors and other officials to restrict the clerics' influence and political activities; hence a covert or even overt struggle between the two.[27]

One such clash occurred between Governor de Mezy and Bishop Laval. There had been disagreement between Laval and Governors d'Argenson and d'Avaugour, and Laval went to France to present his side of the controversy to Louis XIV. While Laval was in France the King asked him to nominate a new governor for New France. Laval proposed an old comrade from the Hermitage of Caen, Chevalier de Mezy, hoping for a friendly relationship with him as governor.[28]

Laval and de Mezy, the new governor, returned to New France together in 1663. However, after a harmonious beginning, they disagreed over the constitution of  the new Sovereign Council. The Council had as its principal members the governor and the bishop who, in the absence of the *intendant,* had to name five other members jointly. Laval, knowing the citizens of Québec better than de Mezy, arranged the selection of  those who favored the Church.[29]

The governor soon realized this , and on February 5, 1664, had a notice posted with the sound of the drum to the effect that for matters regarding the royal service, the petitions to the Council should be addressed directly to the governor and not to the councillors.[30] Laval refused to endorse de Mezy's action and rebuked him from the pulpit. The governor, having no access to the pulpit, again had an ordinance published with the accompaniment of the drum with his version of the quarrel, in which he dismissed three members of the Council and called upon the citizens to select new members to replace them. The dispute continued for months, while the governor and the bishop each using his respective medium of public communication, until the governor fell seriously ill and died on May 5, 1665. But on his deathbed he repented and asked forgiveness from the Church. People were now convinced that God was on the side of the Church.[31]

The conflict between Governor de Mezy and Bishop Laval was not confined to the appointment of members to the Sovereign Council. The sale of liquor to the Indians, which the Church opposed and declared a sin from the pulpit, had been another bone of contention between the two men.[32] Interestingly enough the same issue caused another controversy with another governor.

Shortly after the arrival in 1672 of Frontenac, the glamorous new governor of Québec and Lieutenant-General of Canada, a sermon was given in his presence denouncing the sale of liquor to the Indians, by this time a familiar theme in Québec pulpits, and denying the King's right to intervene in the controversy. Frontenac, who considered the issue purely the concern of the secular authorities, objected to the sermon as a statement against the authority of the king and complained to the priest's superior. The latter disavowed the sermon and attributed the incident to the priest's overzealousness. Frontenac nevertheless warned that if the occasion ever arose again he would put the preacher "where he would learn how he ought to speak" from the pulpit.[33]

Later Frontenac, in his effort to stop the illicit fur trade in Montréal, discovered that the governor of the city was himself the greatest offender and summoned him to Québec. Abbé Fenelon, who considered himself a mediator between the two men, did not approve of Frontenac's high-handedness and arrogance in demoting and imprisoning the Governor of Montréal. He vented his feelings by strongly criticizing Frontenac in an Easter Sunday sermon in 1674. Although the priest's superior repudiated the sermon, a furious Frontenac summoned Abbé Fenelon before the Sovereign Council and later shipped both him and the errant governor of Montréal back to France to stand trial.[34]

Turning to our example of the role of the pulpit in Church — state relations during the British rule beginning in 1759, we should remember first that as a French Canadian institution the Catholic Church was considered to be under the British administration. But with the departure of French officials and prominent citizens, the clergy became the sole custodian of the inhabitants' way of life in a colony ruled by an alien force. Thus the bishops, as prominent citizens, gradually became the natural spokesmen and leaders of French Canada, and their cooperation was deemed necessary for the administration of the colony. In short, the British administrators had to take notice of the Church.[35]

The historical event of interest to our discussion occurred about one hundred and forty years after Frontenac's reported clashes with the Church. At the height of British rule, Governor Sir James Craig, in his effort to stamp out the French Canadian nationalism demonstrated by the growing independence of the House of Assembly and the *Parti canadien*, wanted the Catholic clergy to give up their usual "political neutrality" and openly side with the government.

In February of 1810 Craig for the third time in a row dissolved the House of Assembly. In March he ordered the seizure of the newspaper *Le Canadien* and the imprisonment of its owners and editors. Then in a proclamation he attacked the "seditious and treasonable propaganda" distributed throughout the province. By order of the governor his proclamation was well circulated by the newspapers, the officers of the militia, and the clergy.

To reinforce the secular arm of the government with religious power, the governor sent for the Catholic Bishop Plessis to attend the Executive Council, where the latter was informed of the disaffection against the British government fomented by *Le Canadien*. The governor complained about the apathy and probable sympathy of a large number of the Catholic clergy with this anti-British propaganda. He ordered the Bishop and his clergy to support with all their effort his proclamation, in order to counteract the "seditious propaganda" and teach the people loyalty to the King and obedience of the law.[36]

Bishop Plessis, who had ordered his clergy not to meddle in politics, had to reverse his order and in a pastoral letter praised Craig's paternal tone in the proclamation. He asked all parish priests to read the proclamation publicly and to destroy in their parishioners' minds the ill effects of the "seditious propaganda."

On the 1st of April Plessis, after himself reading the proclamation from the pulpit, launched into a vigorous sermon in which he condemned not only disobedience but even criticism of the government to an audience estimated at eight thousand. His example was followed by numerous priests who preached loyalty to the government in their respective parishes.

Though there were reports that the proclamation was not favorably received in many parishes, the governor now had proof of the power of the pulpit in the efficiency with which the clergy had broadcast his proclamation. Furthermore, the fact that there had been no subsequent outcry against the governor showed the value of support from the pulpit.[37]

Our discussion so far and these three historical examples demonstrate several points. First, from the time when the Catholic Church effectively entered communal life in New France, the pulpit was recognized as a public medium, and officials both ecclesiastical and temporal used it for communication with the people. Second, it is clear that both Church and state authorities took advantage of the pulpit as a propaganda outlet. Of course, the Church was in a more favorable position in this respect because the pulpit was part of its organization and the clergy had control over it.[38] For instance, Governor de Mezy had to resort to placarding accompanied by the beating of a drum to publish his version of the dispute with Bishop Laval, who had rebuked him from the pulpit. The same is true of General Frontenac, who had to resort to force or threat of force when subjected to pulpit publicity unfavorable to him or the state. Third, even in the early 19th century when newspapers had appeared on the scene and were used for political communication, the pulpit was still considered an important medium of public communication. Governor Craig, for instance, was aware of the prestige and pervasive influence of the pulpit among the illiterate rural population in comparison to the press, whose impact was confined to the literate urban elite.[39]

# Canadian Studies in Mass Communication

*The Involvement of the Pulpit in Major Events.* To provide further illustrations of the impact of the pulpit as a medium of public communication we turn next to a discussion of two major historical events — the war between France with Britain which ended French rule in North America in 1763 and is known as the Seven Year War, and the 1834-38 rebellion against the British authorities.

*The Seven Year War and Its Aftermath.* The undeclared world-wide struggle between France and Britain began in North America in 1754 and officially ended with the Treaty of Paris in 1763.[40] Meanwhile, in Canada the almost permanent absence of a bishop from Québec from 1727 to 1740 weakened Church organization and influence, after its apex during the episcopates of Bishops Laval and Saint Vallier.[41] Nevertheless, when Bishop de Pontbriand was consecrated in 1740, he could still make effective use of the pulpit thorugh his pastoral letters to the parish priests. De Pontbriand issued pastoral letters for almost any occasion. For instance, he recorded in a pastoral letter his joy at the appointment of Governor Vaudreuil because of his Canadian origin. He wrote another letter rejoicing in the arrival of General Montcalm to face the British army. During the war not only did he stir Québecers against the British invaders, he also recorded each victory in a separate pastoral letter. Even famine and defeat were occasions for issuing pastoral letters to be read in the parishes throughout the land.[42]

Thus after the surrender of Québec City to the British, in June of 1759 de Pontbriand advised parishioners through a pastoral letter to show a conciliatory and submissive attitude toward the conquerors of religious communities in Québec.[43] In another letter in October of the same year the bishop ordered a public prayer for peace. Of religious communities in Québec he wrote in November to Murray, the British commander, that he hoped they would conduct themselves in such a way that they would not merit any blame and added, "I am recommending that to them explicitly ...."[44]

It is reasonable to assume that at least part of Murray's leniency and consideration toward the conquered population of Québec, and in particular his lack of hostility toward the Catholic Church, was due to Bishop de Pontbriand's (and his successor Briand's) effective use of the pulpit in counselling non-belligerent attitudes and conduct by the population toward the British authorities and troops.[45]

The same policy of supporting the state from the pulpit was followed by the Church in subsequent years. For instance, at the same time that the Québec Act came into effect in May of 1775 (revoking the Proclamation of 1763, which aimed at the assimilation of the French Canadians into an English colony governed under English law), the American Congress was interested in winning the French Canadians to the American side of the conflict with the British. To achieve this goal American agents were actively promoting anti-British feelings in Canada, hoping to prevent the French Canadians from joining the British in armed conflict against America.[46]

Governor Carleton, unsure about French Canadian sentiments, urged Bishop Briand to call his flock to arms. Briand, in a pastoral letter dated May 22 and sent to the districts most open to American influence, justified this call to arms on the ground that England had just granted them "the practice of our laws, the free exercise of our religion, and the privileges and advantages of British subjects." The bishop stressed that the French Canadians were bound by their religion as well as by their oath of allegiance to defend their country and the British King.[47]

Vicar-General Montgolfier of Montréal also backed Carleton in a similar letter to the priests in his domain. Nevertheless, the contagion of Americanism was widespread, and many objected to mobilization because they considered the British-American war merely an Anglo-Saxon family quarrel. Some even criticized the active part taken by the clergy in the British interest. It is reported that while no more than 500 joined the American forces, most desired the capture of Québec by the Americans.[48]

The Québec clergy gradually won the British government's confidence by publicly and consistently showing their loyalty to British rule, not only during the British-American conflict of the 1770's but also during the unrest and disorder of 1793-4 and 1796-7, when anti-British agitation by agents of the revolutionary government of France had reached its greatest height in Québec.[49] For instance, in November of 1793 Bishop Hubert issued a firm pastoral letter declaring that the bond that had attached the French Canadians to France was completely broken, and the loyalty and obedience they had formerly owed the King of France had been transferred to the King of England. In another letter in 1796 the bishop ordered the clergy to impress upon the people how closely they were obliged to maintain themselves in loyalty to the King of Great Britain. Again, when Nelson defeated the French fleet in 1798, Bishop Denaut ordained public thanksgiving for the "good news."[50]

This repeated public support of British rule from the pulpit could not have been without effects. Thus in the 1812 invasion of Canada by the Americans, Vicar-General Deschanaux, in Bishop Plessis' absence, called people to the defence of the country in the name of religion. This time, however, unlike during the American revolution, the population who had illuminated Québec City in honor of Nelson's victory and whose press had called Napoleon "lawless," did not intend to welcome the Americans. Following their Bishop's advice from the pulpit they willingly embraced the British cause. The assembly cheerfully voted the funds and about 6,000 militia were raised without difficulty.[51]

*The Rebellion of 1834-38.* The 1834-38 rebellion against the British administration in Canada was a widespread social movement and the Catholic

**15**

Church was involved in it from the beginning. The *Patriotes* in effect demanded self-government and had declared their wishes through ninety-two resolutions adopted by the Québec Assembly in 1834 which in some ways resembled the American Declaration of Independence.[52]

In response London appointed a royal commission in 1835, headed by Lord Gosford, who was also named as governor, to end the difficulties. The royal commission completed its work in the winter of 1836-7 and its report was on the whole unfavorable to the claims of the Assembly dominated by the *Patriotes*. The decision of the British government regarding its Canadian policy reached Canada in early 1837 and touched off an explosive response. Originally the *Patriotes* intended a passive resistance and economic boycott, but as in the American Revolution, this gradually led to violent opposition.[53]

The newspapers were instrumental in spreading the ideas and the propaganda of the *Patriotes*. For instance, the Declaration of Saint-Ours, which explicitly declared that the Canadians were no longer bound except by force to the English government, and was prepared by the *Patriotes'* Central Committee on May 7 was published in *La Minerve* and the *Vindicator*.[54] Subsequently meetings were held in other towns and the governor and the "vicious" British system were violently attacked by the speakers.[55]

On the other hand, on July 25, at a banquet attended by all the clergy of the diocese honoring the consecration of Bishop Bourget as his coadjutor, Bishop Lartigue of Montréal set the tone for the sermons of the priests under his authority by condemning revolt against legitimate authority and violation of the laws of the land. He also forbade giving absolution to anyone who taught insubordination to the government. The résumé of these bishops' positions was reflected in both loyalist and opposition papers. Bishop Signay of Québec also recommended prudence to his clergy.[56]

Meanwhile Governor Gosford had issued a proclamation attacking the *Patriote* leaders and thus increased the unrest. In August congregations walked out on the traditional *Te Deum* which followed the proclamation from the pulpit of the new monarch Queen Victoria.[57]

The governor's subsequent conciliatory position did not help and the Assembly remained uncooperative. The governor dissolved the Assembly on August 26. More mass meetings followed. Young men took an oath to be faithful to the fatherland and die for its liberation, and military training and resistance to British officials were also urged.[58]

In the midst of these mass meetings controlled by the *Patriotes*, in October Bishop Lartigue issued a pastoral letter condemning rebellion against the established government, which *La Minerve* labelled as "more politics from the pulpit" and "a second edition of Gosford's proclamation." Some people left the church while the bishop's letter was being read from the pulpit and, according to

Wade, 1200 *Patriotes* paraded opposite St. James Cathedral in Montréal. One group greeted Bishop Bourget and the clergy after the mass with the cry of "*A bas le mandement!*" (down with the pastoral letter) or the singing of the *Marseillaise*. The pressure was so intense that Bishop Lartigue offered his resignation to Rome.[59]

Although the condemnation of revolt by Bishop Signay was treated with respect and obeyed in the districts of Québec and Trois-Rivières, it was opposed in Québec City, the capital. In response to a public call for submission to lawful authority from Abbé Baillargeon, the priest of Québec, one *Patriote* newspaper wrote that it would be better for the priests to receive their tithes and the thousand other taxes and preach morals to their followers rather than get involved in political disputes where they were moved by private interests. Another *Patriote* paper attacked the editor of a loyalist paper, who had defended the Québec priests' position, as one "who has betrayed and continues to betray the interests of the country." When open violence broke out attacks were carried out against the Church and priests' property.[60]

By mid-December serious encounters between rebel forces and government troops had occurred, and after loss of lives and property the government forces prevailed. Meanwhile Bishop Signay condemned the insurrection in a pastoral letter on December 11. The priests were also encouraged by the government to calm the people by their sermons.[61]

Interestingly enough the clergy were not all of a single mind. According to Wade, Bishop Bourget was *Patriote*-minded enough to reprimand one priest for his zeal in making himself "a crier or a herald for the state" in his effort to disseminate its message and cool tempers.[62] The priests of Montréal were more sympathetic to the *Patriote* cause and Bishop Lartigue placed one of them under interdict because he had taken an active revolutionary role. This was a priest whose inflammatory preachings in support of the *Patriotes* had offset the preachings of the loyalist clerics and led to another encounter with government troops.[63]

On February 7, 1838, Bishop Signay in a pastoral letter called for thanksgiving at the return of peace and urged unity among various factions. Bishop Lartigue did the same. In general, the intervention of the clergy and the reactionary role they played during the rebellion increased their unpopularity among the people and at any rate failed to dislodge the *Patriotes*, who rose again.[64]

However, the rest of the story is beyond the scope of this paper. It is sufficient to say that in response to the report of Lord Durham, the next British governor, whose aim it was to "elevate the Province of Lower Canada to a thoroughly British character," the prospect of national extinction pushed many moderate French Canadians to join the *Patriotes*, and this time the Catholic clergy did not interfere. As a matter of fact Bishop Lartigue objected to Durham's use of the pulpit to flood the country with his proclamations.

Looking back at the Seven Year War and the rebellion of 1834-38, we see clearly the significant role that the pulpit of the Catholic church played in these monumental events.[65]

By preaching avoidance of confrontation with the British army and recommending to the population a conciliatory attitude after the defeat of France in the Seven Year War, the Catholic clergy not only prevented bloodshed and destruction, but also helped ensure a smooth transition from French to English rule.[66] Through legitimization of the British conquest of 1759 and subsequent support of British policies from the pulpit, the clergy also gradually won the confidence of the British government and became the intermediary between the state and the population, making them the political leaders of the French Canadians.[67]

In these relationships the state and the Church were both clearly aware of the role of the pulpit as a medium of public communication, of information as well as propaganda.

With respect to the rebellion of 1834-38, the public position of the Church, according to Gillis, was cautious at the beginning. It appeared to support the demanded reforms. However, once the "extremists" took over, the movement lost the public support of the Church. Bishop Lartigue of Montréal attacked the *Patriotes*. In response, the reformist *Patriotes* became openly anti-clerical. In return, except for a very few preachers in the urban areas, the clergy exhorted the people to reject armed revolt.[68] The loser in these clashes was the *Patriotes,* who underestimated the propaganda power of the pulpit.

An interesting aspect of the 1834-38 rebellion is the fact that the pulpit was also used by some pro-*Patriote* preachers. This was a case of the pulpit in one parish opposing that in another.[69] Also, the rivalry between the pulpit and the press is worthy of our attention. Except for a small minority of urban preachers the pulpit appears to have been the propaganda arm of the loyalists. The newspapers, on the other hand, were usually *Patriote* organs, (although there were loyalist papers, too) and apparently popular only among the urban literate elite.[70]

While there does not seem to be any evidence of a direct reference to specific persons or newspapers from the pulpit, the newspapers of the time, did not hesitate to mention names in their exchanges with the clergy. All this shows that as a medium of public communication, the pulpit was in many ways similar to, and a perfect match for, the press which was a newcomer in the arena.

*Alternatives to the Pulpit.* So far we have been examining the emergence of the pulpit of the Québec Catholic Church in the pre-Confederation era as a medium of public communication and its involvement in various historical events. A full understanding of the pulpit as a public medium also requires an examination of other contemporary media. We have already discussed the relationship between

**18**

the newspapers and the pulpit early in the nineteenth century. What other media co-existed with the pulpit?

In the earlier days, in addition to the town criers, our report shows the use of placarding, sometimes accompanied by the beating of a drum, by government officials to bring important announcements to the attention of the people. At a more limited level we have also seen that criminals were held in the church courtyard on holidays with placards hanging from their necks which detailed their wrongdoing. However, the use of the crier and placarding were not as established and institutionalized as communication from the pulpit, with its unparalleled organization in terms of time, place and personnel which gave it a unique regularity and permanence. In addition to its prestige, it was the medium with unlimited opportunity to reach almost everybody and transmit complex ideas.[71]

Books, of course, existed in New France. But they were mostly published abroad and their circulation was very limited. Not only was most of the population illiterate, but the few church-affiliated organizations which had collections of books, such as the Sulpician Seminary in Montréal, did not lend their books even to members of their own communities.[72] Thus, except for a very few who had private libraries, most had little access to books. Actually, any book that was not devotional in character was banned. There are reports that the clergy did not hesitate to destroy such books on the spot. There were also certain occasions on which "heretical" publications were publicly burned in the town square.[73]

In general reading and the ownership of books was discouraged.[74] The clergy did not hesitate to express the opinion that literacy and learning of the common man would destroy his faith. Further, the monopoly of the pulpit as an effective medium of public communication was made more complete by the Church's preventing the operation of the printing press.[75]

The Church also sought to control the theatre. Corneille, Racine and short Latin plays had been staged by religious teachers. But when Governor Frontenac arranged for Molière's *Tartuffe* to be played in 1694, this comedy, which lampooned religious zealotry, angered the clergy. Bishop Saint Vallier intervened. The play was stopped and the officer who played the leading role arrested. According to Jaenen, the Bishop's right to denounce the theatre was upheld by the Sorbonne religious authorities in France, but no assistance was offered from the secular arm in enforcing the moral code .[76]

It seems that with increased contact with the outside world (the United States and Europe), increased population, and the emergence of large towns and cities, the control of the Church over rival media gradually took the form of admonitions to the participants, although the dominance of the pulpit as a medium of public communication continued.

*The Components of the Roman Catholic Pulpit as a Medium of Public Communication.* In studying any medium of public communication sociologists make a distinction between channel, audience, content, and source. Let use see if this conceptual framework can be applied to the Catholic pulpit in pre-Confederation Québec, and if the pulpit was different from today's media in this respect.

In his application of these concepts to modern and pre-modern societies Lerner has provided us with  a model for comparison between the two systems.[77] First, while the channel in media systems in modern societies is mediated (by print, transmitted sound and/or pictures), in the oral systems in pre-modern societies it is face-to-face and personal.

Unfortunately, Lerner's lack of historical knowledge and unfamiliarity with the culture of the region he studied have prevented him from making an in-depth examination of the established patterns of communication in these pre-modern societies, and led to his misunderstanding of them.[78] In the case of pre-Confederation Québec, for example, our observation shows that communication via the pulpit in the Roman Catholic Church, although based on face-to-face contact, was not personal, casual and random. It took place at specified places and times and in accordance with prescribed standards. It was highly controlled and enjoyed respect, if not reverence, from its audience. In short, the operation was institutional, and it was this institutional character of the system that guaranteed a regular and rapid diffusion of its message to members of the target population.

## Lerner's Model

|  | Media Systems | Oral Systems |
|---|---|---|
| Channel | Broadcast (mediated) | Personal (face to face) |
| Audience | Heterogeneous (mass) | Primary (groups) |
| Content | Descriptive (news) | Prescriptive (rules) |
| Source | Professional (skill) | Hierarchical (status) |

Turning to the concept of audience, Lerner considers the media systems' audience as heterogeneous and anonymous, whereas in oral systems the audience is said to consist of primary groups. In the case of pre-Confederation Québec, we have already seen that the early parish districts consisted of a number of *rangs*, which did not form a community. Later, when some places had their resident priests, a community relationship developed among the residents, but many non-residents from adjacent *rangs* also attended the Sunday mass. Hence it is doubtful that the relationships between all the members of the pulpit's Sunday audience were very close or that the priest knew everybody intimately. As the population increased, especially in large centers such as Montréal and Québec, homogeneity among the parishioners and intimacy in the relationship between the members of the audience and between them and the clergy decreased further. Interestingly enough, it is exactly in these large population centers that communication via the pulpit reached its peak as a public medium and most resembled the modern mass media in its impact on the development of socio-political issues. Thus on special occasions, when hundreds of people from all walks of life flocked to the church and filled the doorways and courtyard in order to listen to the sermon, anonymity and heterogeneity marked the audience of the pulpit as in the case of the modern media.

The content of communication via the media systems, according to Lerner's model, is descriptive in nature, whereas that of the oral systems is prescriptive. In the case of the Catholic pulpit in pre-Confederation Québec, it is true that the primary function of the sermon was to provide guidance to the faithful by spelling out the appropriate rules of conduct. But it would be misleading to say that the Roman Catholic pulpit in Québec was exclusively concerned with religious matters. It was also used as a medium by which the news was disseminated. More significantly, it served as a medium of communication between the people and their leaders. Government officials were dependent on the Church for this channel of communication, and when a rift between the bishop and the governor prompted the former to cut off the latter's access to the pulpit, the government suffered as a result.

Regarding the involvement of the pulpit in public issues, we should remember that in small parishes the priest was often the only literate and well-informed person among his parishioners. He was thus not only their spiritual leader but also their guide and mentor. Under these conditions his opinion on many questions was sought and respected. Therefore, as their leader and spokesman he expressed his views with respect to many issues of concern, from the pulpit as well as in face-to-face contacts.

On larger issues which were of concern to the Church in general, the bishop communicated his instructions via *mandements* or pastoral letters to all the priests under his authority, who either read them directly or relayed them indirectly from their local pulpits. In this way the Church did not hesitate to express its views via the pulpit during national crises, in opposition to certain segments of society, during elections, and even in rebuttal to the press in later years. It has also been noted that opposing views from the pulpits of different parishes were sometimes expressed, reflecting dissension in the ranks of the clergy.

With respect to source or the communicator, Lerner's model suggests that in media systems he is a professional who has been trained for his role, whereas in oral systems the communicator can be any person of a higher status who instructs and guides his subordinates. Although it is obvious that Catholic priests in pre-Confederation Québec had a higher rank than their audience, at least in the religious realm, and most of their pronouncements were meant and received as guidance, their communication was not always confined to religious instruction, and there are reports that on some occasions the parishioners directly and indirectly disagreed with or opposed the views expressed from the pulpit.[79] Therefore, the need for effective, persuasive communication was recognized by the Church and seminarians studied rhetoric and received training for their role as public communicators.[80] Again, in large parishes there were priests who specialized in giving sermons.

Let us now recapitulate the comparison between the Catholic pulpit in pre-Confederation Québec and the modern mass media in light of Lerner's model. It is obvious that communication via the Catholic pulpit in Québec was not a personal, random activity. It was rather regular and institutional. The audience, at least in the larger towns and in the later years, was heterogeneous. As we come closer to the present, the relationships between the communicator and the audience and among the members of the audience themselves are characterized more and more by anonymity. The news, government edicts, and interpretations thereof were often communicated via the pulpit, and in small parishes in the early days the pulpit was often the only regular contact parishioners had with the outside world. Finally, the priests received training for developing skills in communication, and in larger population centers some even became specialized for the task.

Although the Catholic pulpit and its role have undergone changes during the pre-Confederation period, its many similarities to the modern public media, seem to have increased, especially in later years. As we come nearer to the present time, we see that the audience, content and the communicator of the pulpit resemble more the modern mass media in their characteristics. For instance, although the pulpit still retains some of its original characteristics, such as unmediated face-to-face contact between the communicator and his audience, in other ways there are more similarities between it and the newspaper in the first half of the nineteenth century.

In conclusion we see that the Catholic pulpit in pre-Confederation Québec does not fit comfortably in Lerner's oral systems category because it shows more affinity with his media systems. Further, with the passage of time the pulpit shows more characteristics of a media system, although it never becomes identical with it.

It is such an intermediate position and progression which justifies our considering the Catholic pulpit as a predecessor to the modern mass media.

## POSTSCRIPT

An adequate and well documented study of the role of the Catholic pulpit as a medium of public communication in pre-Confederation French Canada, based on scrutiny of the primary (French) sources by someone who is thoroughly familiar with the history of Canada and with the Catholic faith, has yet to be written. In this preliminary study the objective is rather to highlight an important but neglected function of the pulpit, which is often seen only as an ancillary part of the Church.

Under more favorable conditions the study of the pulpit could be much improved and expanded. For instance, although in the opinion of the author enough evidence has been presented in this paper to demonstrate the function of the Catholic pulpit as a medium of public communication, sometimes the discussion appears to go beyond preaching and sermons to focus on the political action and influence of the Church. In these parts my assumption is that this political action and influence have been mediated by the pulpit. A more satisfactory approach would be for each ecclesiastical order to be individually examined in its historical and social contexts to see if it was read from the pulpit, set the tone for sermons, or posted at the church door, and with what consequences.

The paper also very briefly discusses the training of the clergy in rhetoric and public speaking, and the fact that some priests specialized in preaching. With more resources one could go further into this subject and examine the curricula of the French Canadian seminaries of the time, and possibly compare the specialists with other priests in terms of their social standing and influence among the parishioners. In the sociology of mass communication there is some evidence to support the hypothesis that public exposure via mass media tends to increase one's social visibility and, therefore, prestige and influence in the society.[81] It should be possible to test the same hypothesis with respect to the pulpit in the pre-mass media era.

## NOTES

[*] A paper presented at International Association for Mass Communication Research meetings in Barcelona, Spain (July, 1988).

1. See Philippe Garigue, "Change and Continuity in Rural French Canada," pp. 129, 131; Robert Redfield, "French Canadian Culture in St. Denis," p.61; and Jean-Charles Falardeau, "The Role and Importance of the Church in French Canada," pp. 349-51 in Marcel Rioux and Yves Martin, *French Canadian Society*, Vol. 1, 1971. Also see Cornelius J. Jaenen, *The Role of the Church in New France*, 1976, p. 163; and D.

Hugh Gillis, *Democracy in the Canadas; 1759-1867,* 1951, pp. 35-36, 196, among others.

2. Mack Eastman, *Church and State in Early Canada,* 1915, p. 12; and Mason Wade, *The French Canadians: 1760-1967,* Volume One (1760-1911), 1968, p. 3.

3. Walter Alexander Riddell, *The Rise of Ecclesiastical Control in Quebec,* 1968, pp. 77-78.

4. *Ibid,* pp. 104-105; and Falardeau, *op. cit.,* p. 345.

5. Riddell, *op. cit.,* pp. 100-102; and Wade, *op. cit.,* p. 4.

6. Jaenen, *op. cit.,* p. 42; and Riddell, *op. cit.,* p. 73.

7. Eastman, *op. cit.,* pp. 187-88; and Jaenen, *op. cit.,* pp. 39-47.

8. Jaenen, *op. cit.,* pp. 124, 126-27; and Riddell, *op. cit.,* pp. 106-108. According to Guindon the Catholic Church was the dominant French Canadian institution in New France. See Hubert Guindon, "The Social Evolution of Quebec Reconsidered," in Marcel Rioux and Yves Martin, *op. cit.,* p. 154. For more on Laval see A. Leblond de Brumath, *The Makers of Canada: Bishop Laval,* 1910.

9. Pierre Deffontaines, "The Rang Pattern of Rural Settlement in French Canada," in Marcel Rioux and Yves Martin, *op. cit.,* pp. 3-19. See also Gerald Fortin, "Socio-Cultural Change in an Agricultural Parish," in Marcel Rioux and Yves Martin, *op. cit.,* pp. 92, 94, 96.

10. Jean-Charles Falardeau, "The Seventeenth Century Parish in French Canada," in Marcel Rioux and Yves Martin, *op. cit.,* p. 26.

11. *Ibid.;* and Riddell, *op. cit.,* p. 23. For the number of rural parishes in New France and the ratio of priests to the rural population at various times during the French era see the same source, p. 79.

12. See Wade, *op. cit.,* p. 40; Falardeau, "The Role...," *op. cit.,* p. 346; Garigue, *op. cit.,* p. 134; and Gillis, *op. cit.,* pp. 18-19. In another place Gillis reports that "the Sunday morning homily in the parish church served as a newscast no less than moral injunction." Gillis, *op. cit.,* p. 96. See also Falardeau, "The Seventeenth Century...," *op. cit.,* p. 28.

13. Riddell, *op. cit.,* p. 63. See also Falardeau, "The Seventeenth Century...," *op. cit.,* p. 30; and Garigue, *op. cit.,* p. 128.

14. Wade, *op. cit.,* p. 85, 102; Falardeau, "The Role...," *op. cit.,* p. 345; Jaenen, *op. cit.,* p. 117; and Garigue, *op. cit.,* pp. 130-131.

15. Jaenen, *op. cit.,* pp. 118, 122; Riddell, *op. cit.,* p. 70; and Fortin, *op. cit.,* p. 92. According to Falardeau, the parish and the clergy today still maintain their influence through Sunday mass and the pulpit among many French Canadians, and the bishops' pastoral letters influence the policies of the Quebec government. See Falardeau, "The Role...," *op. cit.,* pp. 352-53, 356.

16. Jaenen, *op. cit.,* pp. 142-43; and Eastman, *op. cit.,* p. 180.

17. Jaenen, *op. cit.,* p. 123.

18. *Ibid.,* p. 154; and Eastman, *op. cit.,* p. 125.

19. Gillis, *op. cit.,* p. 96. For instance, the church also published banns for a proclamation of an intended marriage on three successive Sundays. See Jaenen, *op. cit.,* p. 137.

20. Guindon, *op. cit.,* p. 153. According to a visitor in New France in 1683, "You could neither have a pleasure party nor play at cards nor see the ladies without the curate being informed of it and preaching about it publicly in the pulpit." His zeal went so far as to name individuals. See Eastman, *op. cit.,* p. 219. See also Wade, *op. cit.,* p. 24. It should be remembered that, except in a few larger centers, all the people

worshipped in the same church. Thus the attendance at church represented the whole community. See Riddell, *op. cit.*, pp. 70, 76.

In spite of industrialization and mobility, some believe that even today the Sunday sermons perform some of the same functions for many parishioners. See Falardeau, "The Role...," *op. cit.*, p. 353.

21. In 1717 the captain of the militia, who was a representative of the people as well as an agent of the government, was assigned this duty. His announcements were made from the church steps. See Jaenen, *op. cit.*, pp. 21, 49, 117; and Wade, *op. cit.*, p. 34.

22. See Jaenen, *op. cit.*, pp. 63, 135. See also H.H. Walsh, *The Church in the French Era*, 1966, pp. 200-201.

23. Jaenen, *op. cit.*, p. 123, 143; and Wade, *op. cit.*, p. 165.

24. Jaenen, *op. cit.*, p. 159.

25. See Eastman, *op. cit.*, p. 64; and Riddell, *op. cit.*, p. 115. Since the *habitants* were poor, it often fell to the royal treasury to pay a salary to the Canadian clergy and financially support many parishes; hence the influence of the state. See Riddell, *op. cit.*, pp. 79-80; and Falardeau, "The Seventeenth Century...," *op. cit.*, p. 26.

26. According to Gillis the *intendant* was the third-ranking official in the colony preceded by the governor and the bishop. In practice, however, he became the administrative head of affairs and was quite powerful. See Gillis, *op. cit.*, p. 21. According to Wade he was "charged with judicial, police, financial and economic activity." See Wade, *op. cit.*, p. 33.

27. For example, see Eastman, *op. cit.*, pp. 66, 94, 109-11, 187-88; and Jaenen, *op. cit.*, pp. 39, 46-47. For a different interpretation of this conflict see Gillis, *op. cit.*, pp. 14-19. See also Falardeau, "The Role...," *op. cit.*, pp. 344-45.

28. Eastman, *op. cit.*, pp. 47-48.

29. Jaenen, *op. cit.*, p. 45; and Eastman, *op. cit.*, pp. 50-53.

30. Eighty four years later the people of Montreal heard *Intendant* Bigot's ordinance read to them to the accompaniment of drums in the Market Place, announcing the closing of the city's General Hospital. The custom apparently had continued until the mid-eighteenth century. See Walsh, *op. cit.*, p. 197.

31. See Eastman, *op. cit.*, pp. 50-66; Jaenen, *op. cit.*, pp. 45-46, 142; and Walsh, *op. cit.*, pp. 135-36. For more on de Mezy see Saffray de Mezy in *Dictionary of Canadian Biography*, (henceforth *DCB*), Vol. 1, 1966, pp. 587-590.

32. See Eastman, *op. cit.*, pp. 79-82, 279-80.

33. *Ibid.*, pp. 138-39, 183-84; and Walsh, *op. cit.*, p. 144. During the second governorship of Frontenac (1689-1698), we find the decision of the religious authorities at the Sorbonne in France, which supported the position of Bishop Saint-Vallier in limiting the brandy trade, still being read from the pulpit by the order and in the presence of the bishop in July 1698. Again, on another occasion Saint-Vallier did not hesitate to indirectly criticize in a pastoral letter Frontenac's position regarding the sale of liquor. See Eastman, *op. cit.*, pp. 276-77.

34. See Walsh, *op. cit.*, pp. 145-46; Jaenen, *op. cit.*, pp. 49-50, 122; and Eastman, *op. cit.*, pp. 158-59. For a discussion of another conflict between Frontenac and the Church see the section "Alternatives to the Pulpit" in this paper. For more on Frontenac see Baude de Frontenac et de Palluau in *DCB*, Vol. 1, *op. cit.*, pp. 133-142.

35. See Gillis, *op. cit.*, pp. 35-36; Riddell, *op. cit.*, pp. 132, 147 and Falardeau, "The Role...," p. 346. The influence of the Church and the bishops in particular is clearly reflected in the reports of the British governors and administrators. For instance, see Wade, *op. cit.*, pp. 104, 108, 113; and Gillis, *op. cit.*, p. 100.

36. This action of Craig was not without precedent. During the French era Governor Denonville, in the absence of Laval, sought support from Grand Vicars Berniers and Ango in the 1687 campaign against the Seneca Indians. In his proclamation the governor announced as his aim "the glory of God." At mass all priests were to read the governor's manifesto and the grand vicars exhorted "all true sons of the Church" to second the intention of His Majesty and the governor with all their might in "this holy war." According to Eastman the appeal was a complete success. See Eastman, *op. cit.*, pp. 336-37.

37. For the story of Governor Craig see Jean-Pierre Wallot, "The Lower Canadian Clergy and the Reign of Terror," *Study Sessions*, (The Canadian Catholic Historical Association), No. 40, 1973, pp. 53-60. For more on Craig see Helen Taft Manning, *The Revolt of Canada: 1800-1835*, 1962, pp. 77-94; Wade, *op. cit.*, pp. 104-115; and *DBC*, Vol. V, 1983, pp. 205-213.

38. Guindon emphasizes the superiority of the church over both political and commercial establishments of the time with respect to its communication system. See Guindon, *op. cit.*, p. 153. The extent of the bishop's control over the pulpit as a medium of public communication is very clear from the following examples.

    *Intendant* Talon in October of 1667 complained to Colbert, the Minister of Marine, that Bishop Laval had caused some difficulty over the publication of ordinances from the parish pulpits as provided for in the custom of Paris. In response Louis XIV wrote to Laval to conform to the custom in France by ordering the priests in every parish in Canada to publish from the pulpit all acts of justice rendered by the officers of the Sovereign Council or by ordinary judges. According to Eastman, though obliged to submit, the bishop raised this difficulty more than once in the succeeding years. See Eastman, *op. cit.*, p. 107.

    In December 1681 a Recollet preacher, who spoke in a fashion which did not meet with the approval of Bishop Laval, was reprimanded and removed. See Eastman, *op. cit.*, p. 150.

    On the other hand, the Sovereign Council in 1676, in the Roland case, forbade all churchmen to read in the churches or at the church doors any document except those of a purely religious nature or as ordered by the courts. See Eastman, *op. cit.*, p. 187.

39. Jeremy Cockloft reported in 1811 that the two weekly newspapers in the "dreary Province of Canada" seemed "very weakly productions." Instead the population was more interested in "private gossip." See Wade, *op. cit.*, pp. 118-19. This report shows that the two weeklies that existed at the time did not enjoy a wide circulation.

40. See *Encyclopedia Canadiana*, Vol. 9, 1965, pp. 279-283.

41. Jaenen, *op. cit.*, pp. 57-62.

42. *Ibid.*, p. 63: and Walsh, *op. cit.*, pp. 194, 200-201. When, in 1690, Admiral Phips left Boston to capture the French colony, Bishop Saint-Vallier also called upon the people to fight "the enemies not only of the French people, but of our faith and religion." When Phips was defeated and returned, according to Walsh, all admitted that the clergy had played an important role in sustaining the soldiers and in keeping the people from panic. See Walsh, *op. cit.*, p. 158.

43. See Dubreil de Pontbriand, Henri-Marie in *DCB*, Vol. III, 1974, p. 197; and Riddell, *op. cit.*, p. 158.

44. See *DCB*, Vol. III, *op. cit.*, p. 198.

45. On Murray's attitude toward the colonists' and Briand's stance and pastoral letter see Gillis, *op. cit.*, pp. 28-30, 34-35. See also *DCB*, Vol. III, *op. cit.*, p. 199. For more on Briand see Briand, Jean-Olivier in *DCB*, Vol. IV, 1974, pp. 94-103.

46. See Falardeau, "The Role...," *op. cit.*, p. 347; and Wade, *op. cit.*, pp. 65-68.
47. See the sources in the previous footnote; and *DCB*, Vol. IV, *op. cit.*, p. 101. For more quotations from Briand's pastoral letter on this occasion and the British administration's satisfaction with his support see Riddell, *op. cit.*, pp. 158-162.
48. See Wade, *op. cit.*, pp. 68-69. Gillis reports that at the beginning of the American invasion even some priests gave them a good reception. However, he also reports that in general the clergy were "openly" working against the Americans. See Gillis, *op. cit.*, pp. 86, 90.
49. See Gillis, *op. cit.*, p. 35. The French Revolution of 1789 did not gain support among French Canadians, probably because secularism and new ideas had not yet developed in this citadel of orthodoxy, where educational standards and intellectual attainments were much lower than in France. See Jaenen, *op. cit.*, p. 125. As for the subject of this paper, it would be illogical to expect the Catholic clergy to promote a doctrine which ran counter to their outlook and interests. Hence, there was anti-revolutionary and anti-France propaganda from the Québec pulpits. As a result, the devotion of the people to pre-revolutionary France was maintained. For more on this subject see Gillis, *op. cit.*, pp. 94-97, 105. See also Falardeau, "The Role...," *op. cit.*, pp. 347-50.
50. See Wade, *op. cit.,* pp. 99-100.
51. *Ibid.,* p. 122.
52. For a general discussion of these resolutions see *Ibid.*, pp. 143-44.
53. *Ibid*, pp. 152-59.
54. *Ibid.,* pp. 160-62.
55. *Ibid.,* pp. 162-64.
56. *Ibid.,* p. 164. According to Gillis, Bishop Lartigue issued three pastoral letters between July 1837 and January 1838 condemning the rebels and calling for repentance. See Gillis, *op. cit.*, p. 148.
57. See Wade, *op. cit.*, p. 165.
58. *Ibid.,* pp. 165-67.
59. *Ibid.,* pp. 168-69.
60. *Ibid.,* pp. 169-70.
61. *Ibid.,* pp. 174-76.
62. *Ibid.,* p. 176.
63. *Ibid.,* pp. 176-77. These incidents show that the Catholic clergy were not indifferent to the nationalistic aspirations of the population, but their political leadership also made other demands on them. Hence a series of contradictory stresses. For more on this subject see Garigue, *op. cit.*, pp. 131-132.
64. See Wade, *op. cit..*, p. 179. The conservative outlook of the Catholic church and the dominant role of the pulpit in the political arena became more visible during the 1870s and 1880s, when some bishops exhorted the faithful to vote for men who would protect the church. For instance, when the Liberal Party lost the provincial elections in 1875 against the opposition of most of the clergy, some of the losing Liberals (*'Rouges'*) applied to the courts for annulment of the elections on the grounds of undue influence exercised by the clergy on behalf of the Conservatives (*'Bleus'*). But the role of the pulpit in post-Confederation Quebec is beyond the scope of this paper. For more on this 'Holy War' against the Rouges, which involved Wilfred Laurier and even the Pope in Rome, see Wade, *op. cit.*, pp. 356-70, among others.
65. *Ibid.,* p. 190. The Province of Upper Canada, populated mostly by English-speaking Canadians, was also involved in the rebellion. According to Gillis, the crucial

27

blunder of the rebels there, as in Lower Canada, was their break with the clergy. Egerton Ryerson, the most influential Methodist minister, was a moderate reformer who could rally the people to the cause in that province. See Gillis, *op. cit.*, pp. 149-50. For a delineation of the Provinces of Lower Canada, mostly the settlements of French Canadians, and Upper Canada, see J. Bouchette as cited by Riddell, *op. cit.*, p. 17. For the role of the non-Catholic pulpit during the American Revolution see Asghar Fathi, "The Pulpit as a Medium of Public Communication During the American Revolution," in this same volume.

66. Apparently the failure of the domestic economy during the war also had an influence in weakening resistance to the British. See Gillis, *op. cit.*, pp. 21-23.

67. According to some writers, the ecclesiastical influence of the Roman Catholic Church during the British era was greater than during the latter part of the French rule. See Riddell, *op. cit.*, p. 100; and Jaenen, *op. cit.*, p. 162.

   Unlike France, in New France the secular authorities were involved in parish affairs. Thus, in addition to being an ecclesiastical unit, the parish also became a civil and military unit (See note 21 above). After the conquest the British found the parish organization an effective mechanism for their administration. See Garigue, *op. cit.*, p. 131; Guindon, *op. cit.*, p. 152; and Wade, *op. cit.*, p. 50.

68. Gillis, *op. cit.*, p. 148.

69. *Ibid.* The practice of using the pulpit in feuds between the Catholic clergy in New France went far back. For example, Abbé de Queylus, a Sulpician, denounced the Jesuits as pharisees from his Montreal pulpit just a few years before the arrival of Laval in 1659. See Walsh, *op. cit.*, pp. 103-04; and Wade, *op. cit.*, p. 37.

70. See Guindon, *op. cit.*, p. 152.

71. In 1685 *Intendant* De Meulles reported that the church lacked adequate personnel for the necessary services in the colony. He alleged that "...three quarters of the people at least do not hear mass four times in a year." See Jaenen, *op. cit.*, p. 143. This report shows that at least in the earlier days the pulpit did not reach some people.

72. A report in 1784 says that not a man in five hundred among "Canadian peasants" could read. See Riddell, *op. cit.*, p. 89; and Jaenen, *op. cit.*, p. 133.

73. See Jaenen, *op. cit.*, pp. 132-33; Riddell, *op. cit.*, p. 59; and Wade, *op. cit.*, p. 24.

74. Bishop Laval in 1670 urged that French merchants should be prohibited from sending Protestant clerks to the colony. Among other things that the Bishop feared was their habit of lending heretical books. See Riddell, *op. cit.*, pp. 74-75.The censorship power of the Church was so well established that even in 1892, when the newspaper *Canada Revue* was banned by the Bishop of Montreal, the courts legally recognized this right of the Church. See Fernand Dumont and Guy Rocher, "An Introduction to a Sociology of French Canada," in Marcel Rioux and Yves Martin, *op. cit.*, p. 190.

75. See Jaenen, *op. cit.*, pp. 133-34. According to Wade, no newspaper had been established in Québec under French rule. A friend of Benjamin Franklin named Fleury Mesplet started the first purely French press in Canada in 1776 to disseminate American propaganda. See Wade, *op. cit.*, pp. 53, 72. For a different version of the Mesplet story see W.H. Kesterton, *History of Journalism in Canada*, 1967, p. 5. Even during British rule the language barrier and censorship by the Church shut out everything tending to question the authority of the Church. See Riddell, *op. cit.*, p. 94.

76. Jaenen, *op. cit.*, p. 132. See also Wade, *op. cit.*, p. 25.

77. See Daniel Lerner, *The Passing of Traditional Society*, 1958, pp. 54-56.

78. For a discussion on the applicability of the Lerner's model to the traditional mode of public communication in the Muslim societies see the author's "The Islamic Pulpit as a Medium of Political Communication," *Journal for the Scientific Study of Religion,* 1981, 20(2): 163-172. A discussion of the surprising amount of similarity between the Catholic pulpit in pre-confederation Québec and the Islamic pulpit in the history of the Muslim lands is beyond the scope of this paper.

79. The weakening of the hierarchical relationship between the preacher and his audience, and the non-prescriptive character of the content of his message, is exemplified by an incident in 1757. A priest publicly denounced a couple of his parishioners from the pulpit, and found himself being sued by them. See Jaenen, *op. cit.*, p. 122.

80. At the urging of Laval, classes started in 1659 for the training of priests in administering the sacraments, catechising, and preaching. In 1663 he established the Séminaire de Québec, See Brumath, *op. cit.*, p. 47; Walsh, *op. cit.*, pp. 161-62; Jaenen, *op. cit.*, p. 99; and Wade, *op. cit.*, p. 38.

81. See Charles C. Wright, *Mass Communication: A Sociological Perspective*, 1986, pp. 153-54, among others.

# THE PULPIT AS A MEDIUM OF PUBLIC COMMUNICATION DURING THE AMERICAN REVOLUTION*

*ABSTRACT: This study explores the role of a traditional mode of public communication in an important historical event in North America over two hundred years ago. The evidence supports the hypothesis that the political process is as much influenced by access to the means of communication in a pre-industrial society as it is in modern societies.*

The purpose of this paper is to examine the pulpit as one of the predecessors to mass media in the American society. We want to see if there were periods in the history of this nation when a strong need for public communication was felt; and if so, consider the social institutions which satisfied such a need.

The American Revolution during the latter part of the eighteenth century appears to have been a movement where the leaders felt the need to reach people of different social standings in order to inform and agitate them into action against the British. It also appears that the religious organizations of that period, through the pulpit, provided an effective medium for reaching this wide range of people both in towns and back country.

After the examination of these points the implication of such an endeavor for the study of mass communication will be discussed.

*The American Revolution and The Clergy.* In the year 1740 the English colonies on the Eastern seaboard were in constant fear of the Indian raids, the French Roman Catholics in Canada whose trappers and Jesuit clergy roamed into Western Pennsylvania, northern Ohio and New York, and the Roman Catholic Spaniards in Florida eager to expand northward. From time to time there were clashes between English colonists and their enemies. The longest and bloodiest of these struggles was the French and Indian War which raged throughout the 1750's.[1] It was during this time that Jonathan Mayhew exhorted his Boston parishioners against the infidels. " Do I see the slaves of King Louis with their Indian allies, dispossessing the freeborn subjects of King George of the inheritance received from their forefather...."[2] Thus the clergy preached and aroused the people during that war. As leaders of the colonists they also raised troops and fought battles.[3]

In 1763 the British, at the termination of the Seven Years War according to the Treaty of Paris, acquired the French dominions in Canada and at the same time the Spanish were also driven out of Florida. The new world was open for English expansion.[4] However, the victory had been achieved at a great cost. In order to pay the huge debt incurred during the war and the future expenses of a standing army in America the British Government wanted to tax the colonies. There had been frictions between England and colonies in the past when Britain had passed laws regulating the affairs of the colonies, but this time the colonists were determined to resist. Particularly in New England the temper ran high when they objected to being taxed without their consent. The agitation of the Puritan clergy and some radicals influenced the formation of a band of men called "Sons of Liberty" and British imports were boycotted.[5]

In reaction to these developments in America, the British merchants pressured their parliament into repealing the Stamp Act which had placed a tax on all legal documents, newspapers, diplomas, playing cards, etc. In America, the pulpits resounded with the glad tidings. Tyranny had been defeated and the colonists were delivered from slavery.[6]

Another factor which contributed to the friction between the colonies and the mother country was that for several years a group of New England Anglicans was attempting to strengthen the official religion by bringing bishops to America. This situation not only recreated the memory and fear of lord bishops as the right arm of the crown ready to undercut the colonists liberties, but also raised the question of the British parliament's rights over the colonies again. The same pastors who fought the Stamp Act went to work battling against the introduction of bishops. Pamphlets were written and articles appeared in the weekly papers and hundreds of eloquent sermons were delivered from the pulpits. Loss of religious liberties meant loss of fundamental liberties.[7]

Meanwhile, the British parliament instituted a new series of economic restrictions in place of the abolished Stamp Act. To enforce these laws British troops were billeted in Boston homes. Clashes were bound to occur. In March of 1770, British soldiers fired on a band of roughs who were taunting them, killing five. This "Boston Massacre" was piously magnified by New England devines, Reverend John Lathrop preaching upon the "Innocent Blood Crying to God from the Streets of Boston."[8]

When in 1773 a mob of Bostonians boarded boats loaded with tea to be sold in the colony with the abhorred tax included and dumped the cargo into the sea, the British were infuriated and thus, strict regulations were passed which put Boston and Massachusetts under royal control.[9] Again, the Puritan clergy rallied the people and patriot agitators such as Samuel Adams cried for action.[10]

Event piled upon event and in April of 1775 hostility broke out with the battles of Lexington and Concord.[11] In almost every incident that led to the war the influence of the New England's Puritan Clergy may clearly be seen.[12] During the war, as before, sermons were important in disseminating propaganda. Preachers, as usual, carried the burden of this work during their regular Sunday sermons and again on special occasions such as fast days, election days and anniversaries.[13] For example, the sermons preached on the anniversaries of the Boston massacre and the battle of Lexington directed the entire blame towards George III and the depredations of the British troops. The dissidents' alliance with Catholic France against the British did not endanger the Protestant religion in America. According to the sermons of the time, it was Heaven's special dispensation![14]

In many towns the people, excited by the preachers, assailed British sympathizers. Some New England preachers were accused of putting an end to the Church of England.[15] In one case it is reported that the zeal and energy of a single minister won a whole pro-British town to the American side by his Sunday-after-Sunday preaching of the doctrine of liberty and resistance.[16] Throughout the war the preachers pled for the cause of the union through sacrifice and persistent, united effort.[17] Jonas Clark, for example, in 1781 preached: "O my fathers and bretheren! ALL! all is yet at stake!—All may yet be lost, if we rise not, as one man, to the noble cause!"[18] Others like Charles Chauncy augmented the spirit of their people during days of suffering and discouragement by bringing to the service of the Revolution an invincible confidence in its final triumph. "Our cause is so just," preached he, "that if human effort should fail, a host of angels would be sent to support it."[19] The Puritan preachers also encouraged enlistment and often succeeded where the recruiting officers failed.[20]

Many clergy served as chaplains in the army and often these men were enthusiastic in the cause. For instance, David Avery is reported to have "...served long, encouraging the men with his clear, ringing voice through the weary winter at Valley Forge." Again, in March, 1776, Washington and Putnam wrote to the congregation of an influential and popular preacher asking them to give him up to the army.[21]

The impact of the Puritan preachers on the minds of the colonists was not confined to their propagandist role during the revolutionary war. As we shall see later, in their constant struggle against the encroachment of the British on the colonial affairs, the ministers had already sown the seeds of rebellion many years before the Revolution.

*Press as a Medium of Public Communication During the American Revolution.* There was printing presses in operation in Massachusetts as far back as 1638[22] and the first news sheet appeared in 1689 in Boston.[23] In 1750 fourteen newspapers were published in six colonies.[24] The Stamp Act controversy of 1764-65 affected the colonist emotionally, politically and commercially. The situation had intensified during the war and distribution of news gained significance. On April 19, 1775, the day of the first military actions of the Revolution, there were 37 newspapers in the course of publication[25] and subscriptions had increased.[26] The newspapers not only reported the much sought after news but also fought for colonial economic and political rights. For instance, Thomas Paine's pamphlet

*Common Sense* which had a powerful effect in arousing public opinion against England also appeared in the *Pennsylvania Packet*.[27]

The most popular newspaper during the Revolution was the *Boston Gazette and Country Journal*. Samuel Adams, the well known propagandist of the Revolution, often write for this paper[28] and many of his essays were extensively copied by newspapers in other colonies. This duplication of the popular essays, which was one of the essential features of the newspaper at that time, increased the influence of the piece copied.[29]

The Stamp Act, which taxed the newspaper, had alienated the printers from the British,[30] but in some cases publishers were influenced by the amount of money they were offered by the British government either as salaries or subsidies for printing pro-British newspapers.[31] For instance, a formidable and typographically the finest was the *Boston Chronicle*[32], which, like the New York's *Gazetteer*, succumbed to British monetary influence.[33] According to the *New Jersey Gazette* of July 4, 1781 the British spent $500,000 on American newspapers and pamphlets during the Revolution.[34]

However, the newspapers during the American Revolution had obvious limitations. They consisted of small, badly printed, and expensive sheets which appeared only once a week, and they were handicapped by limited circulation, and poor facilities for distribution. Three to six hundred copies a week was an average sale for a colonial paper at the middle of the century.[35] But the greatest impediment to the successful influence of the newspaper was the large number of illiterates in the population.[36]

*The Pulpit as a Medium of Public Communication during the American Revolution.* Besides the newspaper there were other channels of public communication during the American Revolution. Pamphlets were an effective weapon of political argument among the intellectuals.[37] Broadsides (a single printed sheet often anonymously distributed) were particularly suited to the more radical inflammatory type of propaganda directed to the lower class.[38] Many private letters were also influential agencies of communication passing from hand to hand and sometimes finding their way to the newspapers or orations.[39] The formal addresses devoted to advancing the patriot cause such as those delivered at the anniversaries of the Boston Massacre and speeches in the town and assembly meetings were effective media of public communication.[40]

However, probably a more influential medium of effective propaganda during the Revolution was the pulpit.[41] Preachers were part of a highly venerated institution and had regular contact with their audience.[42] As professionally trained communicators, their eloquence clearly demonstrated the superiority of the oral communication in arousing emotions.[43] Historian Clinton Rossiter speaks of their influence during the turbulent years of 1765-1776 in this way: "The thundering pulpit, which through at least half of the colonial period had been the only significant agency of communication, continued to reach tens of thousands who had no time or urge to read pamphlets and newspapers. While Mayhew, Chauncy, Cooke, and Cooper worked their chief influence in print, the forgotten ministers of hundreds of country churches proved once again the power of the spoken word."[44] Not only the leading thinkers among ministers but literally hundreds of other preachers were discussing resistance, unalienable rights and political consent.[45]

To understand the role of the preachers during the American Revolution one should realize their special position in Colonial America in several ways. First, as Rossiter has indicated, they had been and still were significant agencies of communication. In those days of very limited transportation, few newspapers and no electronic media, the ministers, who read more than most of their neighbors, who attended ministerial conventions, who corresponded with their fellow-ministers and men of other towns and colonies, who had been classmates of the rising lawyers and merchants, were likely to be the major channel through which their parishioners could have any contact with the outside world. As preachers they could reach their parishioners not only on Sundays but also on many special occasions prescribed by the churches or by the colonial assemblies, such as days of fasting, prayer, and thanksgiving. Besides doctrinal sermons, bits of important letters, decisions of ecclesiastical councils, proclamations by the government and other important news items, such as the death of the King, were also disseminated from the pulpit.[46]

Second, in Colonial America the opinion of the clergy on all public matters was weighty and the pulpit was the most important single force for shaping and controlling of public opinion.[47] This was because the pulpit, in addition to providing the news to the parishioners, as the guardian of their faith also interpreted the events similar to the role of editorials in modern newspapers.[48]

In performing this "editorial" function, as far as the relationship between the colonists and the mother country was concerned, the pulpit had sown the seeds of rebellion years before the Revolution. To appreciate this point we should remember that at the beginning in Massachusetts the local church was the backbone of the community and the final authority in all matters to its members.[49] This form of practical theocracy was later modified under the influence of the ideas of intellectual preachers like Thomas Hooker (1586-1647), Roger Williams (1603-1683) and Jonathan Mayhew (1720-1766).[50] In other words, throughout the years, in their struggle against British encroachment on the colonial affairs and in reaction to the autocracy of the churches, some Puritan clergy had developed sophisticated theories about government by consent, religious liberty, and the right of resistance. These ideas had filtered down to the minds of their parishioners by the time of the Revolution.[51] For instance, the parishioners were made aware that the Massachusetts commonwealth had been founded on a compact that was drawn up between their forefathers and the King, and that the breach of this sacred contract constituted not only a violation of the terms of the compact, but also a violation of the laws of God.[52] Therefore, the preachers dogmatized the right and the duty of good Christians to resist such a violation.

In this way, with the help of the preachers, a meaningful political theory for the American Revolution had been created which was related to the facts of life not only in minds of patriot leaders but also, thanks to the pulpit, in minds of the ordinary people.[53]

Finally, as propagandists for advancing the patriotic cause the Puritan preachers had an additional advantage which enabled them to adapt the ideologies behind the Revolution to the popular religious belief. The reason for this unique situation was that from the beginning, the Puritans demanded a learned ministry, and in 1636 they had established the Harvard College for such a purpose.[54] The result was that as a whole the New England clergy at the time of the Revolution were graduates of Harvard and Yale.[55] Therefore, the favourite themes of their sermons often consisted of the philosophy of John Locke and the liberal European writers of the eighteenth century curiously blended with illustrations from the Bible.[56] These sermons in effect were "political preachings."[57]

*The Effectiveness of the Pulpit.* However, notwithstanding all of these sermons, and the liberal political doctrines which they imparted, one may ask whether any heed was given to them. In addition to some pieces of evidence already provided[58] the effectiveness of the preachers as propagandist for the cause of the Revolution can be further ascertained by the fact that revolutionary leaders courted their support. For example, it is reported that "Merchants and other Sons of Liberty" gave a banquet to the ministers in 1770 in Boston.[59] The provincial congress of Massachusetts requested the preachers to "...make the question of the rights of colonies...a topic of the pulpit...."[60] Apparently the men in the Congress knew full well that the eloquence of the clergy was more instrumental than the writings of the Otis and the Adamses in arousing people in New England towns.[61] The same body also acknowledged "...with profound gratitude the public obligation to the ministry, as friends of civil and religious liberty."[62]

Unlike the New England clergy the preachers in other colonies did not have as many opportunities for making public appeals, nor did they have the actual presence of the troops in their midst as did those in Massachusetts in 1774. To give the clergy more opportunities to make public appeals, the civil leaders in these colonies appointed fast and prayer days. The result was effective revolutionary propaganda from the pulpit in the form of political sermons.[63]

Not only the Congregationalist and the Presbyterian, but also Dutch Reformed, and Baptist ministers, fearing the threat of the British interference in their affairs, were overwhelmingly on the side of the Revolution. Lutherans,

German Reformed and even the Catholic minority supported the cause. Some of the Anglican clergy in the south also voiced their support from the pulpit.[64]

The effectiveness of the pulpit as a propaganda outlet was also clearly known to the sympathizers of the British. Thus in 1774 a loyalist lawyer, Daniel Leonard, in an essay accounting for the rapid and alarming growth of the spirit of resistance and later of revolution in America, gave a prominent place to the part then played in the agitation by "our dissenting ministers."[65] Again, Ambrose Serle in 1776, while urging the British government to establish superintendents of the press in different colonies, said: "...next to the indecent harangues of the preachers, none has had a more extensive or stronger influence than the newspapers of the respective colonies."[66] Peter Oliver, an historian of the Revolution in Massachusetts expressed his anger at the success of the American clergy in arousing the people against the British in these words: "As to their Pulpits, many of them were converted into Gutters of Sedition, the Torrents bore down all before them. The Clergy had quite unlearned the Gospel, and had substituted Politicks in its Stead."[67]

It should also be remembered that because of their prestige and experience in oratory, in many non-religious patriotic gatherings Puritan preachers were invited as guest speakers as well.[68]

The Anglican Church as a whole took no official stand until forced to it by the patriots. It was not until 1774 that the Anglican clergy openly attacked the patriots and were soon suppressed. However, most of them carried on their propaganda in print under assumed names.[69]

The fact that those preachers who were antagonistic towards the Revolution lost the privilege of preaching, is another example of the effectiveness of the pulpit and the fear of the patriots about counter propaganda from the pulpit. One of the most impressive examples of high principle and courageous conduct on the part of the loyalist preachers is furnished by Jonathan Boucher. This frank anti-revolutionary Anglican preacher received threatening letters and for more than six months he preached with a pair of loaded pistols lying on the cushion in front of him.[70] Soon after he was forced to leave America in 1775. Later in his "Autobiography" attesting to the great influence of the pulpit during the Revolution he wrote; "In American, as in the Grand Rebellion in England, much execution was done by the sermons."[71]

*Other Possible Propaganda Channels.* Other social institutions were not so adaptable to the uses of the propagandists as the pulpit during the American Revolution. For instance, with respect to schools, according to Davidson, it would have taken a good deal of foresight to make and execute any program of education in patriotic principles before 1774, and after that few could foresee how long the struggle would last. Besides there were no courses in citizenship and no extracurricular activities to provide opportunities for propaganda. However there were anti-British sentiments among the college students at that time.[72]

There were a variety of clubs which brought pressure on their members to endorse the anti-British program. But open attacks required the courage, faith and eloquence not very often found in those clubs. The Masonic lodges were also important organizations in those days. However allegiance to the parent lodge in England and the policy of not taking an open stand on issues hampered their use as propaganda channels.[73]

*Discussion.* Pye describes the mass communication process in modern societies as characterized by a distinct and highly organized system operated by professional communicators, while the communication process in pre-industrial societies is not a distinct system. It is unorganized, is not operated by a class of professional communicators, and is totally reliant on face to face communication. The transitional communication process is described as bifurcated — while part of it operates like a modern system the rest remains traditional.[74]

Unlike Pye and others[75] who assume a distinct dichotomy of traditional and modern systems of communication, this paper attempts to discover the institutional patterns in the pre-industrial societies which, under certain conditions, can assume some of the functions of the mass communication in the urban industrial societies.[76] Our purpose is to test three interrelated hypotheses. The first hypothesis states that during a popular social movement the need for communications to a large number of people increases. The second hypothesis suggests that when the need for such a communication has increased, if the target population or part of it can not be reached because of the lack of modern mass communication technology (such as print and electronic media) or because of its inadequacy, the existing communication patterns within certain institutions of the society would be employed. The third hypothesis indicates that some institutions are more adaptable than others for providing communication outlets in the situations reported in the first and second hypotheses.

Looking at the American Revolution we find some support for these hypotheses. A strong need was felt for communication to the public among both the patriots and the loyalists. Print, in the forms of pamphlets, broadsides and newspapers was avidly and successfully employed by the patriots. The loyalists also were keenly aware of the role of the print as a propaganda mechanism and the British spent large sums of money supporting newspapers and pamphlets.

However, both the patriots and the loyalists were also aware of the limitations of the print. On the other hand, prior to the appearance of the print as a medium of public communication, the pulpit had been performing similar functions for many years. Contrary to the assumption of Pye, the pulpit was a distinct and organized system of communication operated by professional communicators. It was distinct in the sense that although the communication via pulpit was face to face due to the lack of modern techniques, it was not of personal and primary group nature. Since it was organized, it was not a random type of activity. It took place at certain times and places and according to prescribed standards. It was institutional. Finally, the preacher was a professional communicator in the sense that he was trained for the position and he had to attain it according to standards established mostly by other preachers.

In general one can reasonably assume that the control of such an institutionally well established medium as the pulpit made the preachers potentially powerful propaganda agents. This fact plus the long standing conflict between the Puritan clergy and the British government made the preachers more than willing to accept the encouragement and the invitation of the patriot leaders (some of whom were also clergymen) to engage in firey political preachings in the turbulent years of 1763-1781. On the other hand, circumstances did not allow the loyalist and the British to use the pulpit to their own advantage.

Orations, addresses in the town meetings and the colonial assemblies, and the resolutions passed during these gatherings were also effective propaganda, but compared with political sermons they were not as institutionalized and therefore, not as influential. Schools and social clubs proved even less suitable for agitation on a grand scale.

*Conclusion.* Some tentative hypotheses have been set out in this paper for further study by research people in mass communication. Systematic attention paid to the communication structure of various societies in their pre-industrial era in order to understand the development and functions of mass communication as we now know them, if carried out as cross-cultural studies, should enhance the value of these suggested hypotheses.

For instance, one could ask: In the absence of mass communication technology such as radio, in what ways did the instigators and agitators of the French Revolution try to reach their target population? According to Leith, the revolutionary Jacobin leaders used the arts, namely drama, music (songs), painting, sculpture, as well as printed literature in order to indoctrinate and impress the public. But the strong tradition of art for the sake of art, among other factors, tended to interfere with the utilitarian approach to art as a propaganda.[77]

Again, with respect to the pre-industrial societies of the twentieth century, one can pose the question: What institutional patterns in various societies have performed the functions of the mass communication during a popular movement and with what consequences? In the case of the Constitutional Revolution in Iran (1905-1909), due to the long standing conflict between the clergy and state, at the beginning the pulpit was most effectively used by the Constitutionalists. However, because most of the clergy did not understand the constitutional form of government and, as the movement unfolded some found it against their own interests, the pulpit could not maintain its effectiveness as a medium of public communication for the cause of the revolution.[78]

# NOTES

\* A paper presented at Pacific Sociological Association annual meetings in San Diego, California (April, 1976).

1. Brauer, Jerald C., *Protestantism in America*, (Philadelphia, no date) pp. 63-4. See also James T. Adams, *Revolutionary New England*, (Boston, 1923), pp. 221-249.
2. Brauer, *op.cit.*, p. 64.
3. *Ibid*, p. 65.
4. *Ibid*; and Adams, *op.cit.*, pp. 278-279.
5. Brauer, *op.cit.*, pp. 65-67; Adams, *op.cit.*, pp. 304-337; and Philip Davidson, *Propaganda and The American Revolution* (Chapel Hill, 1941), pp. 65-82.
6. Brauer, *op.cit.*, p. 67; Adams, *op.cit.*, pp. 338-339; and Alan Heimert, *Religion and The American Mind*, (Cambridge, Mass., 1966), p. 244 and p. 352.
7. Brauer, *op.cit.*, pp. 67-68; Clifton E. Olmstead, *History of Religion in the United States*, (Englewood Cliffs, 1960), p. 1963; Moses C. Tyler, *The Literary History of the American Revolution*, Vol. I (1957) pp. 133-135; and Adams, *op.cit.*, p. 359-360.
8. Brauer, *op.cit.*, p. 68; Adams, *op.cit.*, pp. 349-379; Claud H. Van Tyne, "Influence of the Clergy and of Religious and Sectarian Forces, on The American Revolution," *American Historical Review*, 19:53(1913); and Davidson, *op.cit.*, p. 204.
9. Brauer, *op.cit.*, pp. 68-69; and Adams, *op.cit.*, pp. 388-396.
10. Brauer, *op.cit.*, p. 69; Davidson, *op.cit.*, p. 204; and Edwin Emery and Henry Ladd Smith, *The Press and America* (New York, 1954), pp. 98-104. Although not directly related to the subject of this paper, it seems necessary to specify the identity of the "patriots" during the American Revolution. In addition to the Puritan clergy these consisted of the fairly well-to-do element in the colonial society such as assembly men, country politicians, judges, lawyers and other professional men, and in the North, merchants, and in the South, the planters. It was primarily the interests of the well-to-do which were served by the Revolution. By 1750 they were in virtual control of the colonial affairs. Through their assemblies they had successfully limited the authority of the appointed governors. The British were left primarily with the control of the foreign affairs. This privileged position was seriously endangered after 1763. It appeared that the British government was determined to regain its complete authority over the American colonies. Davidson, *op.cit.*, pp. 31-32, and Emery and Smith, *op.cit.*, pp. 86-90.
11. Brauer, *op.cit.*, p. 69 and Adams, *op.cit.*, pp. 416-420.
12. Van Tyne, *op.cit.*, p. 54.
13. Headley, J. T., *Chaplains and Clergy of the Revolution*, (Springfield, Mass., 1861)
14. Davidson, *op.cit.*, pp. 204-205, and pp. 389-390.
15. Baldwin, Alice M., *The New England Clergy and The American Revolution* (New York, 1965), p. 158 and Charles Mampoteng, "The New England Anglican Clergy in the American Revolution," *Historical Magazine of the Protestant Episcopal Church'*, 9:267-304 (1940).
16. Baldwin, *op.cit.*, pp. 159-160.

17. *Ibid.*, p. 164.
18. Davidson, *op.cit.*, pp. 389-390.
19. Tyler, *op.cit.*, Vol. II, pp. 279-280.
20. Baldwin, *op.cit.*, p. 126 and p. 163.
21. Headley, *op.cit.*, and Baldwin, *op.cit.*, p. 161.
22. Emery and Smith, *op.cit.*, p. 29; and Schlesinger, Arthur M., *Prelude to Independence, The Newspaper War on Britain*, 1764-1776 (New York, 1958) p. 51.
23. Emery and Smith, *op.cit.*, pp. 38-39; and Sidney Kobre, *The Development of American Journalism* (Dubuque, 1969) p. 9.
24. Emery and Smith, *op.cit.*, p. 66.
25. Frank L. Mott, *American Journalism* (New York, 1966) p. 95.
26. Kobre, *op.cit.*, p. 60.
27. *Ibid*, pp. 88-89; and Schlesinger, *op.cit.*, pp. 46 and 253.
28. Adams, *op.cit.*, p. 374; Schlesinger, *op.cit.*, p. 92; and many other places in both of these sources; and Davidson, *op.cit.*, pp. 227-228.
29. Davidson, *op.cit.*, pp. 244-245.
30. Emery and Smith, *op.cit.*, p. 87.
31. Kobre, *op.cit.*, pp. 71-73.
32. Schlesinger, *op.cit.*, pp. 103-108.
33. Kobre, *op.cit*, p. 71. Schlesinger reports that some patriot newspapers were also supported by the popularly elected legislative branch. Schlesinger, *op.cit.*, p. 286.
34. Kobre, *op.cit.*, p.71
35. Schlesinger, *op.cit.*, pp. 58-59; and Davidson, *op.cit.*, pp. 225-226. In the height of the conflict with Britain some papers claimed a circulation of two thousand or more. See Davidson, *op.cit.*, p. 226; Schlesinger, *op.cit.*, p. 54 and pp. 303-304; and Mott, *op.cit.*, pp. 59, 75 & 78.
36. Cullen's argument based on quotations from patriots such as Benjamin Franklin, John Adams and others to the effect that the majority of the Americans at that time could read, does not appear to be convincing. A more objective assessment seems to come from Rutland who, while attesting to the fact that literacy rate in northern colonies, particularly in New England was much higher than in Europe, (p. 7) still reports the considerable rate of illiteracy, along with small circulation and inefficient means for distribution, as major impediments facing the colonial newspaper (p. 22). According to the same source in mid-eighteen century "...only about one American in a hundred was literate and interested enough, had access to, and could pay for a newspaper printed in America." (pp. 33-34) See Maurice R. Cullen Jr. "Middle-Class Democracy and the Press in Colonial America," *Journalism Quarterly*, 46:531-535 (1969); and Robert A Rutland, *The Newsmongers* (New York, 1973). For another source which reports that those able to read in America at that time made up but a small part of the total population see Sidney Kobre, *The Development of the Colonial Newspaper* (Gloucester, Mass., 1960), p. 167. See also Mott, *op.cit.*, pp. 4-5.
37. Schlesinger, *op.cit.*, pp. 44-45; and Davidson, *op.cit.*, pp. 214-216.
38. Schlesinger, *op.cit.*, p. 44; and Davidson, *op.cit.*, pp. 216-218.
39. Rossiter, Clinton, *The Seedtime of the Republic* (New York, 1953) p. 331.
40. Davidson, *op.cit.*, pp. 194-202.
41. Baldwin, *op.cit.*, P. XI. According to historian Rossiter "Had ministers been the only spokesmen of the rebellion, had Jefferson, the Adamses, and Otis never appeared in print, the political thought of the Revolution would have followed almost exactly the same line...." Rossiter, *op.cit.*, p. 328. Van Tyne also reports that "...the pulpit was

in that day the most direct and effectual way of reaching the masses — far out-rivalling the newspapers, then only in its infancy." Van Tyne, *op.cit.*, p. 54, and p. 64. For a similar observation see also Headley, *op.cit.*, p. 23.

42. Although according to Adams the power and the prestige of the New England clergy had declined by mid eighteenth century, "Religion had been too deeply stamped upon New England consciousness for it not to remain one of the leading factors in the life of the people, as to thought, custom and prejudices...." Adams, *op.cit.*, p. 173. See also John Wingate Thornton, *The Pulpit of The American Revolution*, (New York, 1860), pp. xxxv-xxxvi; and William W. Sweet, *The History of Religion in America*, (Evanston, 1950), p. 176.

43. The superiority of the pulpit in this respect was well known to John Adams, a patriot leader and a revolutionary propagandist (and later President of the United States) who sent explicit instructions through his wife to his own minister in Braintree: "Does Mr. Wibird preach against oppression and other cardinal vices of the time. Tell him the clergy here of every denomination...thunder and lighten every Sabbath. They pray for Boston and Massachusetts. They thank God...for our remarkable successes. They pray for the American Army." Davidson, *op.cit.*, p. 93. See also Heimert, *op.cit.*, p. 20. James Otis another prominent propagandist also declared his inability to carry his points without the aid of the preachers. Tyler, *op.cit*, Vol. II, p. 278. See also Van Tyne, *op.cit.*, pp. 48-49.

44. Rossiter, *op.cit.*, p. 330.

45. *Ibid.*, p. 328, and Headley, *op.cit.*, p. 17. Heimert distinguishes between the liberal and the Calvinist preachers' audiences. The former reached a less numerous but also a less humble group of citizens. Heimert, *op.cit.*, pp. 445-448 and pp. 473-476.

46. Baldwin, *op.cit.*, p. 4-5. See also Robert Baird, *Religion in The United States of America* (London, 1844) p. 412.

47. Sweet, *op.cit.*, p. 176; Olmstead, *op.cit.*, p. 194; and Tyler, *op.cit.*, Vol. II, p. 278.

48. Tyler, *op.cit.*, Vol I, p. 132.

49. Baird, *op.cit.*, pp. 180-188; Headley, *op.cit.*, p. 16; and Brauer, *op.cit.*, p.25.

50. For short biographies of these men and their ideas see Rossiter, *op.cit.*

51. *Ibid*, p. 149; Van Tyne, *op.cit.*, p. 52; and Brauer, *op.cit.*, pp. 69-71.

52. Van Tyne, *op.cit.*, pp. 48-50; Brauer, *op.cit.*, pp. 66-67; and Heimert, *op.cit.*, p. 241.

53. Baldwin, *op. cit.*, p. xii. Actually this work intends to show that the New England clergy had popularized the political theory behind the American Revolution long before 1763. See also Van Tyne, *op.cit.*, pp. 48-49; and Heimert, *op.cit.*, pp. 16-18.

54. Brauer, *op.cit.*, pp. 25-26.

55. Sweet, *op.cit.*, p. 176; and Thronton, *op.cit.*, p. xxxiv.

56. Baldwin, *op.cit.*, pp. 7-8; Olmstead, *op.cit.*, p. 194; Thornton, *op.cit.*, pp. xxxiii-xxxiv.

57. Thornton, *op.cit.*, p. vix. This source is a collection of political sermons which "...presents examples of the politico-theological phase of the conflict for American independence...." Van Tyne also reports that "...after 1750 the sermons were listened to as a source of political instruction...they discussed the origin, nature, and end of government, and the rights of man..." *op.cit.*, p. 55. See also Headley, *op.cit.*, pp. 22-23.

58. See footnotes 40, 42 and 56 above.

59. Van Tyne, *op.cit.*, p. 55.

60. Baldwin, *op.cit.*, p. 123; and Rossiter, *op.cit.*, p. 330. Headley reports that: "...pulpit was a recognized power...and its aid formally and earnestly invoked." *op.cit.*, p. III.

61. Headley, *op.cit.*, p. 23; and Rossiter, *op.cit.*, p. 330. See also footnote 43 above. John Adams has entered an item in his diary under "1773. March 5th.Friday," which

shows the popularity of the pulpit and the nature of its audience: "Heard an Oration, at Mr. Hunts Meeting House, by Dr. Benja. Church, in Commemoration of the Massacre in Kings Streets, 3 years ago. That large church was filled and crowded in every Pew, Seat, Alley and Gallery, by an Audience of several thousands of people of all ages and Characters and of both sexes." L. H. Butterfield, (ed.), *Diary and Autobiography of John Adams*, Vol. 2 Diary (1771-1781) (Cambridge, 1962) p. 79.

62. Van Tyne, op.cit., p. 55.
63. Davidson, *op.cit.*, p. 206.
64. Sweet, *op.cit.*, pp. 176-188; Olmstead, *op.cit.*, pp. 194-209; and Davidson, *op.cit.*, p. 207.
65. Tyler, *op.cit.*, Vol. II, p. 278. As a specific example illustrating the immediate impact of the political sermons, Van Tyne reports that: "On August 25, 1765 Mayhew [attacking the Stamp Act] preached from the text: 'I would they were even cut off which trouble you.' When, soon after, a mob destroyed [lieutenant governor] Hutchinson's house, a ringleader, wh was seized, is said to have excused his action on the ground that he was excited by the sermon." Van Tyne, *op.cit.*, pp. 52-53.
66. Davidson, *op.cit.*, p. 333. Schlesinger rejects the secondary role assigned to the press by Serle, see Schlesinger, *op.cit.*, pp. 284-285. Tyler, on the other hand, gives a subordinate place to the newspapers of that time. Tyler, *op.cit.*, Vol. 1, pp. 17-19.
67. Rossiter, *op.cit.*, p. 329.
68. Davidson, *op.cit.*, p. 23 and pp. 202-204; and Baldwin, *op.cit.*, p. 119 and pp. 125-126. Many learned preachers also published their sermons and wrote pamphlets and essays for the newspapers. Again, election sermons which were delivered at the invitation of the governors and later the colonial assemblies were often published and distributed. Thus the influence of the preachers went beyond the spoken word. But the influence of the clergy via print is beyond the scope of this paper. See Baldwin, *op.cit.*, pp. 114-116 and pp. 155-158; Davidson, *op.cit.*, pp. 23-25, p. 209 and p. 216; and Sweet, *op.cit.*, pp. 176-177. For a discussion on the contents and impact of these printed sermons see Headley, *op.cit.*, and Baldwin, *op.cit.*, among others.
69. Davidson, *op.cit.*, p. 299.
70. Tyler, *op.cit.*, Vol. 1, pp. 316-319.
71. Tyler, *op.cit.*, Vol. II, p. 278.
72. Davidson, *op.cit.*, pp. 97-98.
73. *Ibid.*, pp. 99-101.
74. Pye, Lucian W., *Communication and Political Development* (Princeton, 1963) pp. 24-29.
75. For instance, see Daniel Lerner's study of the mass communication in the Middle East which ignores indigenous institutions and history, *The Passing of the Traditional Society* (Glencoe, 1958).
76. For a discussion of functions of mass communication see Charles R. Wright, "Functional Analysis and Mass Communication," *Public Opinion Quarterly* 24: 605-620 (1960).
77. Leith, James A., *The Idea of Arts as Propaganda in France*, 1750-1799 (Toronto, 1965) p. 159. Also see James A. Leith, *Media and Revolution,* (Toronto, 1968); and Charles Hughes, "Music of the French Revolution," *Science and Society* 4:190-210 (1940).
78. Fathi, Asghar, "Communication and Tradition in Revolution: The Role of the Islamic Pulpit," *Journal of Communication*, 29: 102-106 (1979).

# SECTION II

# MASS MEDIA AND SOCIAL CONTROL

# MASS MEDIA AND A MOSLEM IMMIGRANT COMMUNITY IN CANADA*

## Résumé

Le Principal but de cet article eszt de développer un ensemble d'hypothéses, plus ou moins rigoureusement reliées entre elles et fondées sur une analyse fonctionnelle, au sujet du type d'utilisation des *mass media* par un groupe ethnique immigrant doté d'un système culturel et linguistique très différent de celui du pays industriel où ils sont établis.

Les résultats de cette recherche exploratoire semblent indiquer une dépendance très limitée des *mass media* du pays où ce groupe réside, mais un contact persistant avec les programmes sur ondes courtes diffusés de leur lieu d'origine.

On analyse les conséquences de cette situation sur l'immigrant, la communauté ethnique et le pays de résidence. Finalement, on présente les implications de cette situation pour la survivance de communautés ethniques dans leur pays d'adoption.

This paper is about the pattern of mass media use and its consequences by Moslem Arab immigrants in a Canadian city.

The paper consists of two parts. The first part deals with empirical findings based on standardized interviews with 51 Moslem and 22 Christian Arab male immigrant residents of the Prairie City regarding their use of shortwave radio broadcasts from abroad and the Canadian mass media.

In the second part an attempt is made to organize a framework, based on functional analysis, into which can be fitted a variety of hypotheses about the consequences of mass media use by an ethnic group such as the Moslem Arabs in a modern industrial society. But before mass media use by Moslem Arabs is examined, some background information is necessary.

*The Moslem Arab Community.* There were approximately sixty Moslem Arab families in the Canadian Prairie City at the time of the study. Of the 51 household heads interviewed, 92% had come from Lebanon. Seventy-eight percent had been in Canada for 2-14 years, and 12% had been residents longer. Fifty-one percent were under 30 years of age and 76% were married. Most of these Moslem Arabs were manual workers (41% unskilled, 41% skilled, 4% white collar, 4% unemployed, 6% attending schools, and 4% retired). With respect to education, only 12% of the respondents had finished high school.

The center of community life for Moslem Arabs in the Prairie City was a mosque established a few years prior to the study in a small, old building (previously used as a church). The Moslem Association ran the business affairs of the mosque through an elected council. Religious services were conducted on Sundays by a trained religious leader, or imam sent by the Egyptian government. He also conducted a combination "Sunday school" and Arabic language class for children before services. On special religious holidays the people would gather in the mosque hall after the service to eat Arabic food while listening to Arabic music.

The imam appeared to be the leader of the community, not only because of his religious training, but also for his superior education and good command of the English language.

The Moslem Arab immigrants in the Prairie City were part of a larger group — Arab immigrants. The non-Moslem or Christian Arabs, while in contact with Moslem Arabs, were largely considered outsiders. Of the 22 household heads contacted, 82% were Lebanese, 64% had been in Canada between 2-14 years, and 10% had been residents longer. They were more educated and had a higher socioeconomic status (41% had a high school education or higher, and 23 % had white collar occupations). In general, Christian Arab immigrants appeared to be more assimilated in Canada than Moslem Arabs. The data on Christian Arabs are reported in this paper to help produce a sharper picture by providing a basis for comparison.

## I. THE PATTERN OF MASS MEDIA USE BY MOSLEM ARAB IMMIGRANTS

Examination of the pattern of Moslem Arab immigrant use of mass media indicated heavy exposure to Arabic radio broadcasts from abroad and limited exposure to Canadian mass media. In the present section these two points will be considered.

Table I[**] shows that almost all Arab immigrants in the Prairie City listen to Arabic programs from shortwave radio, and Moslem Arabs listen to these programs even more frequently.[1]

In response to the question, "Why did you start listening to Arabic radio programs from abroad?" Table II reveals some interesting reasons such as attachments to the mother tongue and home country, hearing the news because the subject understood only Arabic, and because the subject thought the Arabic stations to be more reliable. On this last point Table III very clearly shows that among Moslems foreign Arabic stations are more credible than Canadian ones.[2]

_____

[**] Tables and charts are at the end of the chapter.

When asked about favorite shortwave radio programs, the responses in Table IV show that Moslems are more evenly divided among the different programs than are Christians who seem to be primarily interested in news and in the Arabic music. Religious Moslem programs (i.e., recitation from the Koran) naturally appeal only to Moslems.

Table V reveals the occasions which Arab immigrants are most interested in listening on shortwave Arabic radio. These are national and religious holidays, and when an Arab leader speaks.

Table VI shows that both Moslem and Christian Arab immigrants in Canada rely mainly on Arabic shortwave radio programs in learning about new Arabic songs.

Listening to Arabic radio programs is definitely a social activity which brings Arab immigrants together as indicated in Table VII. To a lesser degree it provides subjects for discussion among Arabs, and even between Arabs and non-Arab Canadians according to Table VIII.

The subjects were asked if their children should listen to Arabic programs from shortwave radios and why. Table IX clearly indicates that nearly 90% of both Moslem and Christian Arab immigrants want their children to learn the language and culture of their parents.

The tape recorder provides another link with "home" among Arab immigrants. According to Table X, 53% of Moslems and 48% of Christian Arab immigrants own tape recorders; and Arabic music and Koran recitals are among the most favored tapes. But tape listening is not restricted to those who own a tape recorder. Whether an owner or not, 77% (N=49) of Moslems and 81% (N=21) of Christian Arabs listen to other people's Arabic tapes.

In response to the question, "How often do you listen to Arabic tapes?" Table XI shows that tape listening is quite popular especially among Moslem Arabs, and Table XII reveals that listening to Arabic tapes creates occasion for interaction with other Arabs. Finally, when asked should their children be exposed to Arabic tapes 94% (N=49) of Moslems and 95% (N=20) of Christians answered in the affirmative.

The evidence presented so far shows the Arabic programs from abroad, either directly, or indirectly with the aid of the tape recorder, play an important role in the lives of Arab immigrants, particulary Arab Moslems.

*Exposure to the Canadian Mass Media.* With respect to the radio in Canadian mass media, 92.2% (N=51) of Moslems and 91% (N=22) of Christian Arab immigrants listen to local Canadian radio programs. When asked how much time is spent listening to local stations Table XIII reveals that Moslems spend less time than Christian Arab immigrants.[3] Table XIV shows that the major attraction of Canadian radio for Moslem immigrants is the news, while Christian Arabs appear to divide their attention among a variety of programs. When asked with whom subjects discussed local radio programs, Table XV gives evidence that the majority of Moslems do not engage in any discussion. The data show that more Christian (55%, N=20) than Moslem (33.3%, N=48) Arab immigrants buy products advertised on local radios. Moslems seem to rely more on non-mass media channels such as other people or ads in the store windows to find out about sales according to Table XVI.

With respect to T.V., 90% (N=49) of Moslems and 86% (N=21) of Christians have a set at home.[4] But according to Table XVII we see Moslems, more than Christians, prefer "escape" programs. When asked if subjects buy products advertised on T.V., 35% (N=49) of Moslems and 65% (N=20) of Christians answered affirmatively.

Only three persons regularly received a daily local paper among Moslem Arabs.[5]

Comparing foreign and Canadian mass media, it appears that Moslem Arab immigrants are less dependent on Canadian mass media than are Christian Arab immigrants. For example, Moslems seem more to trust Arabic broadcasts from abroad for world news, they do not appear to enjoy western music as much as Christian Arabs, and shop with less guidance from advertisements.[6]

## II. PARTIAL FUNCTIONAL INVENTORY FOR MASS MEDIA USE BY MOSLEM ARAB IMMIGRANTS

The limited data in the first part of this paper seem to suggest that the pattern of mass media use among Moslem Arab immigrants is worthy of special attention. Now it is time the consequences of such behavior be looked at to provide a framework for a systematic approach to the study of mass media use by an ethnic group such as Moslem Arabs. The emerging framework also helps organize the findings reported in the first part of the paper.

In the attempt to organize a framework about the consequences of mass media use by the Arab Moslems C.R. Wright's scheme (Wright, 1960) is followed. Following Lasswell, C.R. Wright distinguishes four areas of mass communicated activities (Lasswell, 1948). *Surveillance*, the collection and distribution of information concerning events in the environment, "Thus corresponding approximately to what is popularly conceived as the handling of news." *Correlation* includes the interpretation of information about the environment and prescriptions for conduct, commonly called editorials. *Transmission of culture* refers to the communication of a group's store of social norms, information, values and the like from one generation to another, or from members of a group to newcomers. Finally, *entertainment* refers to a communication intended to amuse people.[7]

In his scheme Wright following Merton makes a distinction between manifest and latent functions: the intended and unintended consequences for an activity. He also separates function from dysfunction: helpful consequences from harmful ones (Merton, 1957).[8] Considering these factors, Wright then examines the way mass communicated activities affect the normal operation, adaptation, or adjustment of four systems: individuals, sub-groups, social, and cultural systems (1960).

In this paper Wright's scheme will be followed except that the systems under examination are the individual Moslem Arabs, the Moslem Arab Community, and the Canadian Society. The scheme is used to answer two questions. The first question concerning the exposure to Arabic programs by shortwave radio can be formulated in the following manner:

|                  |     |                   |     |              |                |
|------------------|-----|-------------------|-----|--------------|----------------|
|                  | 1.  | manifest          | 3.  | functions    |                |
| What are the     |     |                   |     |              |                |
|                  |     | and               |     | and          | of the Arabic  |
|                  | 2.  | latent            | 4.  | dysfunctions |                |
| shortwave radio  | 5.  | surveillance (news) |   |              |                |
|                  | 6.  | correlation (editorial activity) | | |           |
|                  | 7.  | cultural transmission |  |              |                |
|                  | 8.  | entertainment, from abroad | |         |                |
| for              | 9.  | the individual Moslem Arab immigrants | | |         |
|                  | 10. | the Moslem Arab Community | |          |                |
|                  | 11. | and the Canadian Society? | |          |                |

The second question that deals with the consequences of limited exposure to Canadian mass communicated activities by Moslem Arab immigrants can be presented according to the same pattern with a minor modification (i.e., replacing the phrase "Arabic broadcast" by "the Canadian mass media"). The accompanying charts in which the elements of the above formula are transformed into categories present some of the proposed consequences of mass media use by Moslem Arab immigrant.

These charts can only be of demonstrative value. A complete list of functions and dysfunctions of exposure by Moslem Arab immigrants to shortwave radio programs or limited exposure to Canadian mass media can not be undertaken at this stage. However, a discussion of the limited content of these charts probably helps demonstrate the utility of the approach.

*Functional Analysis of Exposure to Arabic Broadcasts from Abroad.*
Beginning with Chart I, let us consider what it means to the individual Moslem
Arab immigrant, Arab Moslem community, and the Canadian society to have
available news in Arabic via shortwave radio. The positive consequences or
functions for the individual immigrant are several. Firstly, he becomes aware of
the major events in the Arab world or at "home."[9] These news items of much
interest are not often accessible to him by any other means. Secondly, even with
respect to world news, shortwave programs are often superior to Canadian radio
because the immigrant understands his own native tongue better than English and
probably trusts Arabic sources more.[10] A third function of exposure to the Arabic
news via shortwave radio is to bestow prestige upon those who make an effort to
keep themselves informed about events at "home." In the language of sociology of
mass communication they often become "opinion leaders" in matters of the
"home" country (Katz and Lazarsfeld 1955; and Merton, 1957: 387-420). The
fourth function of exposure to Arabic news for the individual immigrant, according
to Chart I, is the feeling of security and psychological satisfaction which results
from being in touch with the "home" culture.[11] Finally, exposure to the same news
from different sources (i.e., world news by shortwave radio and Canadian mass
media) may enable the individual to see events from several perspectives and thus
develop a more objective point of view.[12]

A significant function of exposure to Arabic news via shortwave radio by
Moslem Arab immigrants for the Moslem Arab community is the legitimization of
the ethnic culture in the eyes of its members. For example, Arabic language can
maintain its prestige because English is not the only language used by the mass
media. Again, the Moslem Arab listener is able to develop a sense of pride because
the interests of the English speaking Christian Westerners are not the only ones
expounded and propagated to the world. The cause of the Arabs and Islam can be
aired too.

What are the positive consequences of exposure of Moslem Arab
immigrants to Arabic news from abroad for Canadian society? If these immigrants
are also exposed to news broadcasted by local mass media, the result would be
more sophisticated citizens for Canada. Firstly, knowledge about the events of
another country as well as Canada would produce better informed citizens.
Secondly, as indicated previously, exposure to the same news from different
sources can produce a more objective world view.[13] Further, Canadian society
would be enriched through the information about other cultures, as well as the
possible growth and adaptability of the Canadian culture as a result of such
contacts.[14]

The availability of Arabic news from abroad also presents negative
consequences or dysfunctions. The individual Moslem Arab immigrant in Canada,
to the extent that he is less dependent on Canadian mass media would be less

available for assimilation into the society of his adoption.[15] He may not learn the language as quickly, and consequently may take longer to acquire a knowledge of the Canadian way of life. For the Canadian society news from a foreign source in such a situation would interfere with successful acculturation of its new citizens.

The second mass communicated activity under consideration in Chart I is correlation. According to C.R. Wright, raw news may overwhelm the individual and lead to anxiety. Editorial selection, interpretation, and prescription help prevent this. Again, correlation through organization and interrelating different news items helps the audience digest the news (Wright 1960). What are the functions and dysfunctions of correlation provided by Arabic shortwave radio programs? For the individual Moslem Arab immigrant it has the helpful consequence of enabling him to digest news about the "home" country. It also impedes possible anxiety about the fate of relatives and the home country.

For the Moslem Arab community in Canada the editorial activity of the Arabic shortwave radio programs produces and reinforces solidarity within the ethnic community by reminding its members of the social and cultural bonds that tie them together.[16] For the Canadian society, these editorials result in decreasing the extent of homogeneity and conformity in the society by attracting the attention of Arab Moslem immigrants to non-Canadian issues and by giving different interpretations or prescriptions.[17] If "mass society," being characterized by herd-like behavior where the masses uncritically conform to directions and prescriptions is undesirable (Mills, 1959; Josephson and Josephson, 1962:9-53), then the existence of segments of the society which are not influenced in the same way can be considered an advantage (Porter, 1967:72).

With respect to the dysfunctions of correlation, or the editorial activity of Arabic shortwave radio stations, since the individual Moslem Arab immigrant would stimulate his allegiance to the old country and the Arabic radio editorials would thus reinforce his marginality in the Canadian society,[18] therefore, his integration into the Canadian society becomes problematic. For the Canadian society such a situation has the undesirable consequence of hindering social cohesion, i.e., the society would be handicapped in promoting concern about public issues, or in developing solidarity in response to national emergencies. The third mass communicated activity in Chart I is cultural transmission or the communication of a group's store of social norms, information, and values from one generation to another, or from members of one group to newcomers. For the individual Moslem Arab immigrant this activity by shortwave radio has the advantage of reinforcing the already internalized values and norms, and giving him additional psychic support by continuing socialization according to these values and norms even after his emigration from the fatherland.[19] The Moslem Arab community also would benefit from cultural transmission by Arabic radio programs because they aid socialization of the young and continue socialization of the adult members according to the ethnic culture of the community.[20] For the Canadian society such a situation would produce and reinforce the existing variety of cultures. Thus, Canada would be able to maintain its pluralistic character (Porter, 1967: 68-73) and would less suffer from the problems that afflict a mass society (Vidich and Bensman, 1958; Josephson and Josephson, 1962; and Klapp, 1969). Again, cultural transmission via foreign radio programs for the Canadian immigrant has another advantage for Canada. The immigrant in his contact with other Canadians may relay to them new ideas, practices, or information thus helping cultural growth in terms of diffusion of cultural elements into the society.[21]

The transmission of Arabic norms and values by shortwave radio programs, like any social phenomena, often has dysfunctions as well. For the individual Moslem Arab immigrant it is dysfunctional because it contributes to idiosyncratic behavior in his adopted country by reinforcing and implanting in him norms and values which are incongruent with those of Canada.[22] This situation, of course, hinders the integration of the immigrant into Canadian society.

Although the transmission of Moslem Arabic culture, as indicated, has the function of supporting the ethnic Moslem Arab way of life in the Moslem Arab community, it also has the dysfunction of fostering prejudice against the community by other Canadians. This is because cultural transmission via shortwave radio tends to maintain the gap between the Moslem Arab way of life and the North American Christian norms and values. As far as the Canadian society is concerned, all this impedes cultural consensus. By cultural consensus we mean similarity of norms and values which unify a nation.

The final mass communicated activity is entertainment. The obvious functions of such an activity by Arabic shortwave radio for the individual Moslem Arab immigrant in Canada is to provide respite.[23] Although the T.V. is very popular among the Moslem Arab immigrants as an entertainment medium, it can not provide the range and types of respite they are used to (e.g., Arabic music). Canadian radio is even less helpful than T.V. in this respect.[24] Thus for music, "meaningful" dramas, and religious programs, Moslem Arab immigrants turn to foreign Arabic radio programs.[25] In this way the inadequate supply of entertainment by the Canadian mass media is supplemented directly by heavy reliance on the shortwave radio or indirectly by taping the desired broadcasts, such as recitation of the Koran or new Arabic songs.[26]

This heavy exposure to Arabic entertainment provides the Moslem Arab community in Canada with an additional factor for cohesion by bringing to the attention of its members another bond that ties them together. When one considers the fact that entertainment via mass media is often a group activity and seldom an individual one, the community spirit and group affiliations which are fostered on these occasions seem to provide still another element in support of social cohesion among the Arabs and within the Moslem Arab community in Canada.[27]

For Canadian society the Arabic entertainment provided by shortwave radio programs for Moslem Arab immigrants produces a situation where "mass culture" would not be as likely to develop. Mass culture is defined here as standardized mass production of mediocre cultural products with an emphasis on marketability of these products. One particular area of concern affecting mass society is the consequences accompanying mass culture on the general level of taste (Lowenthal, 1950; Coser, 1960; and Kaplan, 1967).

As for the dysfunctions of entertainment provided by shortwave Arabic programs for the Moslem Arab individual, one can state that it is another factor hindering his integration into Canadian society. The more a Moslem Arab immigrant is exposed to the non-Canadian content of Arabic radio programs (and as a consequence the less time he has for Canadian mass media),[28] the more he remains alien to the Canadian way of life, be it music, language, or politics.

Again, with respect to Canadian society, exposure to non-Canadian entertainment by its immigrant citizens is another area of activity which is incongruent with the Canadian way of life and consequently another wedge in the unity and solidarity among Canada's citizens.

In discussing some of the functions and dysfunctions of exposure to foreign Arabic radio programs for Moslem Arab immigrants in Canada, it should be noted that although for analytical purposes one can separate surveillance, correlation, cultural transmission and entertainment activities, or the individual, the community, and the society, but in actual life situations these separations are unrealistic. For instance, news, editorials, cultural transmission, and entertainment by Arabic shortwave radio all tend to buttress the social organization of the Moslem Arab community, and such a reinforcement also tends to foster the prejudice against the Moslem Arab community by the rest of the Canadians. Again, from another point of view, although the surveillance activity of mass media is concerned primarily with dissemination of the news and information, a certain amount of cultural transmission also takes place in the process. The same is also true of editorial activity and entertainment.

*Functional Analysis of Limited Exposure to Canadian Mass Media.* The previous discussion of Chart I has outlined the consequences of exposure to foreign Arabic radio programs for the Moslem Arab immigrant. Chart II deals with the consequences of limited or lack of exposure of these immigrants to the Canadian mass media. It can be argued that the consequences in both cases are more or less the same in the sense that exposure to non-Canadian mass media would have the same results as lack of exposure to the Canadian media. For instance, listening to foreign Arabic shortwave radio and lack of exposure to the Canadian mass media both have similar consequences in terms of hindering the assimilation of immigrants and impeding cultural consensus in Canadian society. This assertion is basically true, but there are notable exceptions. These exceptions warrant the presentation and discussion of Chart II. The entries in Chart II that are similar to those in Chart I will not be considered. The special consequences that emanate from limited exposure to the Canadian mass media are concentrated upon.

In the area of surveillance or news activity, one of the possible functions of limited exposure to local news for the individual Moslem Arab immigrant in Canada[29] would be his immunity to narcotization. Lazarsfeld and Merton hypothesize that access to mass-communicated news might lead to the unhealthy belief that the individual may think an informed citizen is equivalent to an active one (Lazarsfeld and Merton, 1948). Because of limited exposure to the news from Canadian mass media, Moslem Arab immigrants would not develop such a belief. In other words, they assess their own situation realistically as one of inactive Canadian citizenship.

With respect to the dysfunction of not being adequately exposed to the surveillance activity of Canadian mass media, one can think of the problem that the Moslem Arab immigrant faces by not being as quickly alerted against danger in times of emergency as other Canadians. Again, if one agrees with writers who consider mass media a tool for daily living in urban industrial societies, or the instrumental function of the media, the Moslem Arab immigrant is also handicapped due to the lack of information about weather, road conditions, sales, etc. In all these occasions immigrants have to rely on inefficient pre-mass media devices such as friends, flyers and signs in stores.[30]

For the Canadian society, lack of, or limited exposure to the surveillance activity of local media by Moslem Arab immigrants would create problems in warning the citizens about imminent threats and dangers such as epidemics or natural disasters, because certain segments of the population can not be reached quickly. Regarding the instrumental function, there would also be difficulty in reaching everybody in the target population regarding situations such as traffic control by the police or in sales by department stores.[31] In the area of correlation or editorial activity, one of the functions of lack of exposure to Canadian mass media by Moslem Arab immigrants is that they would not be influenced by the interpretations or prescriptions coached in terms of possible interests of a power elite (Mills, 1959). By not developing the habit of someone else evaluating the situation and charting a course of action for the rest (Mills, 1959), the Moslem Arab immigrant would be in a better position of maintaining his critical faculty.[32]

However, limited exposure to the editorial activities from local mass media would put the Moslem Arab immigrants in a problematic situation because they could not be guided and helped in times of emergency. In such situations they would have no choice but to fall back on pre-mass media devices such as advice and assistance of neighbours and acquaintances. Again, lack of exposure to interpretation and prescription of local media by the immigrants may create undue anxiety in the latter who may misinterpret a rumor or simply panic when somehow forewarned of an emergency without any evaluation or guidance available. For the Canadian society this state of affairs produces problems of coordination and mobilization in times of crisis.

With respect to cultural transmission activity of Canadian mass media, lack of exposure by the Moslem Arab immigrant to nominally Christian North American norms and values would have the function of reducing the probability of his experiencing role conflict. The Moslem Arab immigrant, knowing only on set of behavior standards, would not be under as much cross pressure as when dealing with two sets of conflicting standards (i.e., the Moslem Arab and Christian North American) equally applicable to the situation.

As indicated earlier, the rest of the entries in Chart II are more or less similar to those of Chart I, and do not need further discussion.[33]

## CONCLUSION

The primary aim of this paper has been to develop a set of approximately interrelated hypotheses based on functional analysis about the pattern of mass media use by an ethnic immigrant group with a cultural and linguistic background very different from that of the industrial host country.

A complete list of functions and dysfunctions of exposure by Moslem Arab immigrants to foreign Arabic radio broadcasts and their limited exposure to Canadian mass media is not possible at the present stage. Also, the small number of subjects does not provide adequate information for generalization. However, there seems to be some support for the proposed hypotheses which encourages and warrants further investigation.

In addition to the above objective, this paper also tends to question the notion of future society possessing a high degree of conformity and homogeneity.

In sociological literature of thirty years ago the industrial urban societies were considered as consisting of atomized, unrelated individuals uprooted from their social moorings and at the mercy of mass media. The impact of the media was assumed to be direct and effective — hypodermic needle model (Blumer, 1946). Sociological researchers of later years have demonstrated that even in urban industrial areas most people are well anchored to groups, and group affiliation plays an important role in the behavior of the audience of mass media (Friedson, 1953; and Katz and Lazarsfeld, 1955).

However, concepts such as "mass society," "mass behavior," and "mass culture" still persist in literature (Bell, 1961; and Josephson and Josephson, 1962: 151-199). Often writers who "predict" future society to be a "mass society" characterized by a high degree of conformity, decrease in originality, loss of critical faculty, and low level of taste, refer to mass media as one of the significant "causes," (Rosenberg, 1957; and Macdonald, 1962).

This paper takes a different point of view. According to the study, it seems that with the increase in cross-national and cross-cultural contacts due to advances in communication technology (i.e., the communication satellite), at least in a pluralistic society such as Canada the fear of "massification" is not well founded. The study seems to suggest the hypothesis that unlike the situation of minority ethnic groups and immigrants of fifty years ago and previous, the language and culture of the ethnic communities of today and tomorrow are less in danger of extinction. If it is true that every group desires to maintain and perpetuate its social heritage, and the advance of communication technology greatly facilitates contact between people of similar cultures, separated by distance, it reasonably follows that the chance for the survival of distinct ethnic communities is better today and in the future than in the past.[34]

TABLE I: TIME SPENT WITH ARABIC RADIO STATIONS

| Amount of time | Moslems | Christians |
|---|---|---|
| Every night if possible | 35% | 14% |
| 3 -4 times a week | 17 | -- |
| Less than 3 times a week | 46 | 86 |
| Does not listen | 2 | -- |
| N | 48 | 21 |

TABLE II: REASONS FOR STARTING TO LISTEN TO ARABIC RADIO
STATIONS

| Reason | Moslems | Christians |
|---|---|---|
| to hear home news, attachment to language and home | 53% | 76% |
| To hear news because only understands Arabic | 18 | 05 |
| To hear news and music | 05 | 05 |
| News from Arabic station more reliable | 05 | -- |
| Liked programs | 11 | 14 |
| Ambiguous response | 08 | -- |
| N | 38 | 21 |

TABLE III: CREDIBILITY OF CANADIAN VS. ARABIC RADIO STATIONS

| Believes more | Moslems | Christians |
|---|---|---|
| Eqyptian Cairo radio | 55% | 11% |
| Canadian radios | 28 | 44 |
| Would not believe either | 12 | 39 |
| Compares and makes own inference | 05 | 06 |
| N | 42 | 18 |

## TABLE IV: FAVORITE ARABIC RADIO PROGRAMS

| Type of Program | Moslems | Christians |
|---|---|---|
| Like all same | 08% | 07% |
| News | 34 | 40 |
| Music | 04 | 13 |
| News and music | 21 | 40 |
| News and religious ⁄ | 25 | -- |
| Religious, news, and music | 07 | -- |
| N | 48 | 15 |

## TABLE V: WHEN MOST INTERESTED IN LISTENING TO ARABIC RADIO STATIONS

| Occasion | Moslems | Christians |
|---|---|---|
| Moslem religious holidays | 24% | --% |
| National holidays of country of origin | 18 | 48 |
| When an Arab leader speaks | 49 | 52 |
| Both Moslem religious holidays and national holidays | 09 | -- |
| N | 45 | 21 |

## TABLE VI: SOURCE OF KNOWLEDGE ABOUT NEW ARABIC SONGS

| Learned from | Moslems | Christians |
|---|---|---|
| Friends in Canada | 22% | 14% |
| Friends or relatives back home | 11 | 33 |
| Shortwave Arabic radio stations | 50 | 38 |
| Tapes, records sent from home | 04 | 05 |
| Arabic newspapers | 02 | -- |
| Not interested in songs | 04 | 05 |
| Do not hear new songs | 07 | 05 |
| N | 45 | 21 |

## TABLE VII: WITH WHOM ARABIC RADIO STATIONS LISTENED

| Persons listen with | Moslems | Christians |
|---|---|---|
| Alone | 13% | 14% |
| Arab Moslems | 30 | 05 |
| Arab Christians | -- | 33 |
| Both Arab Moslems and Christians | 53 | 48 |
| Non-Arabs | 02 | -- |
| Do not listen | 02 | -- |
| N | 47 | 21 |

## TABLE VIII: ARABIC RADIO PROGRAMS DISCUSSED

| Discussed with | Moslems | Christians |
|---|---|---|
| No one | 47% | 57% |
| Arab Moslems | 14 | 05 |
| Arab Christians | -- | -- |
| Arab Moslems and Arab Christians | 19 | 33 |
| Canadians | 08 | 05 |
| Canadians and Arabs | 12 | -- |
| N | 49 | 21 |

## TABLE IX: SHOULD CHILDREN LISTEN TO ARABIC RADIO PROGRAMS?

| Should Children listen | Moslems | Christians |
|---|---|---|
| No | --% | --% |
| Not unless they want to | 05 | -- |
| Yes, to learn and/or retain the Arabic langauge | 49 | 63 |
| Yes, to learn about their parents' country | 31 | 19 |
| Yes, to learn about the language and country of their parents | 08 | 06 |
| Don't understand | 05 | 06 |
| Up to the children | -- | 06 |
| Yes, they would enjoy it | 02 | -- |
| N | 39 | 16 |

## TABLE X: CONTENT OF TAPES OWNED

| Content | Moslems | Christians |
|---|---|---|
| Do not own a tape recorder | 47% | 52% |
| Arabic music | 06 | 19 |
| Arabic and Canadian music | 08 | 14 |
| Koran | 06 | -- |
| Arabic Music and Koran | 16 | -- |
| Baby's voice and/or family parties | 10 | 10 |
| Baby's voice, Arabic music | 04 | 05 |
| Others | 02 | -- |
| N | 49 | 21 |

## TABLE XI: HOW OFTEN ARE ARABIC TAPES LISTENED TO

| Amount of time | Moslems | Christians |
|---|---|---|
| Three to four times a week | 65% | 45% |
| Once a week | 22 | 20 |
| Once a month | 09 | 10 |
| Less than once a month | 04 | 25 |
| N | 45 | 20 |

## TABLE XII: WITH WHOM ARE ARABIC TAPES LISTENED

| Persons listened with | Moslems | Christians |
|---|---|---|
| Alone | 07% | --% |
| Other Arab Moslems | 25 | -- |
| Other Arab Christians | -- | 15 |
| Both Arab Moslems and Christians | 59 | 75 |
| Non-Arab | 02 | 05 |
| Arabs and Canadians | 07 | -- |
| Arabs, Pakistanis and Canadians | -- | 05 |
| N | 44 | 20 |

TABLE XIII: TIME SPENT WITH CANADIAN RADIO STATIONS

| Amount of Time | Moslems | Christians |
|---|---|---|
| 3 hours a day or more | 15% | 25% |
| Between 1-2 hours a day | 30 | 25 |
| Less than 1 hour a day | 55 | 50 |
| N | 47 | 20 |

TABLE XIV: PROGRAMS LISTENED TO ON CANADIAN RADIO
STATIONS

| Type of program | Moslems | Christians |
|---|---|---|
| Music | 02% | 10% |
| News | 49 | 15 |
| Talks | 02 | 05 |
| Music and News | 30 | 25 |
| News and talks | 06 | 10 |
| Music, news, talks and commercials | 07 | 35 |
| Others | 04 | -- |
| N | 47 | 20 |

TABLE XV: CANADIAN RADIO PROGRAMS DISCUSSED

| Discussed with | Moslems | Christians |
|---|---|---|
| Nobody | 57% | 30% |
| Arab Moslems | 02 | -- |
| Arab Christians | -- | -- |
| Arab Moslems and Arab Christians | 04 | 10 |
| Canadians | 20 | 50 |
| Canadians and Arabs | 08 | 10 |
| N | 48 | 20 |

### TABLE XVI:  SOURCE OF INFORMATION OF SALES

| Source of Information | Moslems | Christians |
|---|---|---|
| Other people | 04% | --% |
| Newspaper | 27 | 35 |
| Radio | 02 | -- |
| T.V. | 06 | -- |
| Newspaper, radio or T.V. | 40 | 45 |
| Flyers in the mail | 02 | -- |
| Children | 02 | -- |
| Ads in store windows | 04 | 10 |
| Mass Media and other people | 09 | 05 |
| Do not hear of sales | 04 | 05 |
| N | 48 | 20 |

### TABLE XVII:  FAVORITE T.V. PROGRAMS

| Type of Program | Moslems | Christians |
|---|---|---|
| Do not remember the name | 19% | 21% |
| Escape shows (e.g., Lucy, Untouchables) | 56 | 37 |
| Non-escape shows (e.g., news, sports, and/or documentaries) | 15 | 05 |
| Combination of escape and non-escape | 10 | 37 |
| N | 48 | 19 |

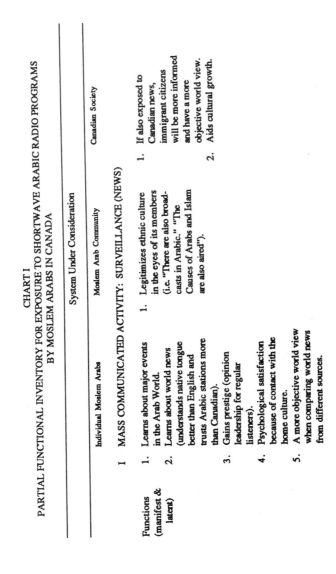

CHART I
PARTIAL FUNCTIONAL INVENTORY FOR EXPOSURE TO SHORTWAVE ARABIC RADIO PROGRAMS
BY MOSLEM ARABS IN CANADA

System Under Consideration

| Individual Moslem Arabs | Moslem Arab Community | Canadian Society |
|---|---|---|
| I MASS COMMUNICATED ACTIVITY: SURVEILLANCE (NEWS) | | |
| Functions (manifest & latent) | | |
| 1. Learns about major events in the Arab World. | 1. Legitimizes ethnic culture in the eyes of its members (i.e. "There are also broad-casts in Arabic." "The Causes of Arabs and Islam are also aired"). | 1. If also exposed to Canadian news, immigrant citizens will be more informed and have a more objective world view. |
| 2. Learns about world news (understands native tongue better than English and trusts Arabic stations more than Canadian). | | 2. Aids cultural growth. |
| 3. Gains prestige (opinion leadership for regular listeners). | | |
| 4. Psychological satisfaction because of contact with the home culture. | | |
| 5. A more objective world view when comparing world news from different sources. | | |

CHART I (Cont'd)
PARTIAL FUNCTIONAL INVENTORY FOR EXPOSURE TO SHORTWAVE ARABIC RADIO PROGRAMS
BY MOSLEM ARABS IN CANADA

System Under Consideration

| | Individual Moslem Arabs | Moslem Arab Community | Canadian Society |
|---|---|---|---|
| Dysfunctions (manifest & latent) | 1. To the extent that needs are satisfied by S.W.R. (e.g. world news), becomes less dependent on local mass media & (1) may not try to learn the language of adopted country & (2) may not learn the ways of country of adoption. | | 1. Impedes efficient acculturation of immigrants. |
| II | MASS COMMUNICATED ACTIVITY: CORRELATION (EDITORAL SELECTION, INTERPRETATION, AND PRESECRIPTION) | | |
| Functions (manifest & latent) | 1. Provides efficiency in assimilating news about the old country. | 1. Produces solidarity within the ethnic community (by reminding members of the social bonds that unify them). | 1. Decreases social conformism. |
| | 2. Impedes anxiety about the fate of relatives and the country of origin. | | |

64

CHART I (Cont'd)

PARTIAL FUNCTIONAL INVENTORY FOR EXPOSURE TO SHORTWAVE ARABIC RADIO PROGRAMS BY MOSLEM ARABS IN CANADA

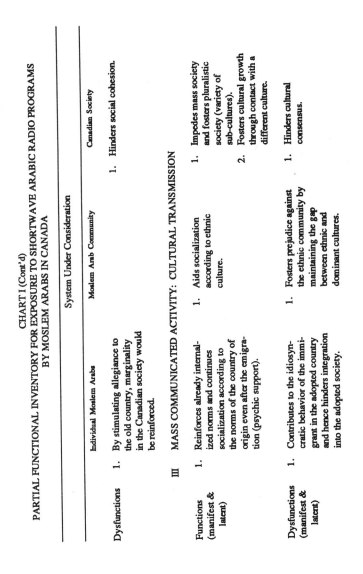

| | System Under Consideration | | |
| --- | --- | --- | --- |
| | Individual Moslem Arabs | Moslem Arab Community | Canadian Society |
| Dysfunctions | 1. By stimulating allegiance to the old country, marginality in the Canadian society would be reinforced. | | 1. Hinders social cohesion. |
| III MASS COMMUNICATED ACTIVITY: CULTURAL TRANSMISSION | | | |
| Functions (manifest & latent) | 1. Reinforces already internalized norms and continues socialization according to the norms of the country of origin even after the emigration (psychic support). | 1. Aids socialization according to ethnic culture. | 1. Impedes mass society and fosters pluralistic society (variety of sub-cultures). 2. Fosters cultural growth through contact with a different culture. |
| Dysfunctions (manifest & latent) | 1. Contributes to the idiosyncratic behavior of the immigrant in the adopted country and hence hinders integration into the adopted society. | 1. Fosters prejudice against the ethnic community by maintaining the gap between ethnic and dominant cultures. | 1. Hinders cultural consensus. |

CHART I (cont'd)

PARTIAL FUNCTIONAL INVENTORY FOR EXPOSURE TO SHORTWAVE ARABIC RADIO PROGRAMS
BY MOSLEM ARABS IN CANADA

| | System Under Consideration | | |
|---|---|---|---|
| | Individual Moslem Arabs | Moslem Arab Community | Canadian Society |
| IV | MASS COMMUNICATED ACTIVITY: ENTERTAINMENT | | |
| Functions (manifest & latent) | 1. Respite (not adequately provided by Canadian mass media). | 1. Provides another factor for cohesion within the community. <br> 2. Fosters solidarity by bringing community members together. | 1. Develops aesthetics (by preventing the emergence of "mass culture"). |
| Dysfunctions (manifest & latent) | 1. Another factor hindering integration into the adopted society. | | 1. Another factor hindering social cohesion. |

CHART II

PARTIAL FUNCTIONAL INVENTORY FOR SUB-NORMAL EXPOSURE TO THE CANADIAN MASS MEDIA
BY MOSLEM ARABS IN CANADA

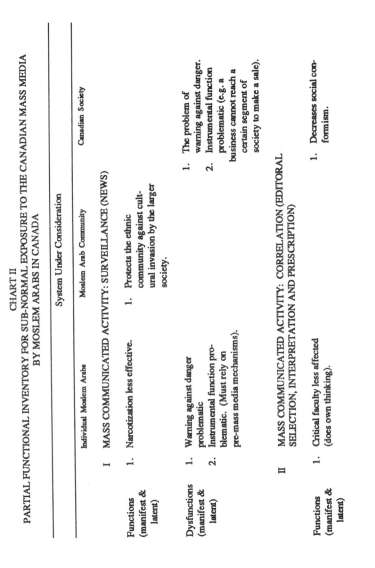

|  | System Under Consideration | | |
|---|---|---|---|
|  | Individual Moslem Arabs | Moslem Arab Community | Canadian Society |
| **I** | **MASS COMMUNICATED ACTIVITY: SURVEILLANCE (NEWS)** | | |
| Functions (manifest & latent) | 1. Narcotization less effective. | 1. Protects the ethnic community against cultural invasion by the larger society. |  |
| Dysfunctions (manifest & latent) | 1. Warning against danger problematic<br>2. Instrumental function problematic. (Must rely on pre-mass media mechanisms). |  | 1. The problem of warning against danger.<br>2. Instrumental function problematic (e.g. a business cannot reach a certain segment of society to make a sale). |
| **II** | **MASS COMMUNICATED ACTIVITY: CORRELATION (EDITORIAL SELECTION, INTERPRETATION AND PRESCRIPTION)** | | |
| Functions (manifest & latent) | 1. Critical faculty less affected (does own thinking). |  | 1. Decreases social conformism. |

67

CHART II (Cont'd)
PARTIAL FUNCTIONAL INVENTORY FOR SUB-NORMAL EXPOSURE TO THE CANADIAN MASS MEDIA
BY MOSLEM ARABS IN CANADA

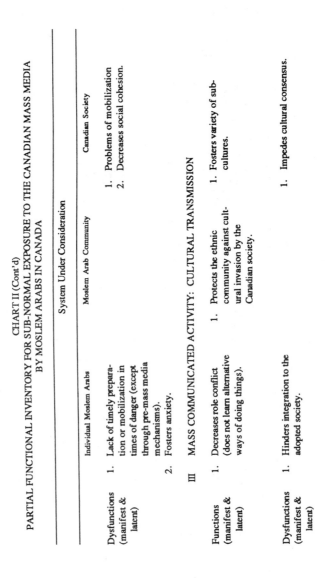

| | System Under Consideration | | |
| --- | --- | --- | --- |
| | Individual Moslem Arabs | Moslem Arab Community | Canadian Society |
| Dysfunctions (manifest & latent) | 1. Lack of timely preparation or mobilization in times of danger (except through pre-mass media mechanisms). 2. Fosters anxiety. | | 1. Problems of mobilization 2. Decreases social cohesion. |
| III | MASS COMMUNICATED ACTIVITY: CULTURAL TRANSMISSION | | |
| Functions (manifest & latent) | 1. Decreases role conflict (does not learn alternative ways of doing things). | 1. Protects the ethnic community against cultural invasion by the Canadian society. | 1. Fosters variety of subcultures. |
| Dysfunctions (manifest & latent) | 1. Hinders integration to the adopted society. | | 1. Impedes cultural consensus. |

68

Mass Media and a Moslem Immigrant Community in Canada

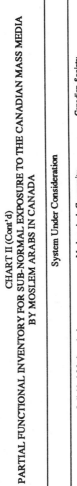

CHART II (Cont'd)
PARTIAL FUNCTIONAL INVENTORY FOR SUB-NORMAL EXPOSURE TO THE CANADIAN MASS MEDIA
BY MOSLEM ARABS IN CANADA

System Under Consideration

| Individual Moslem Arabs | Moslem Arab Community | Canadian Society |
|---|---|---|
| | IV  MASS COMMUNICATED ACTIVITY:  ENTERTAINMENT | |

Functions (manifest & latent)

1. Protects the ethnic community against cultural invasion by the Canadian society.

1. Fosters diversity of tastes (weakens "popular culture").

Dysfunctions (manifest & latent)

1. Hinders integration.

69

# Canadian Studies in Mass Communication

# NOTES

\*  Reprinted from ANTHROPOLOGICA, N.S. Vol XV, No. 2, 1973, pp. 201-230.
   I wish to thank Carole L. Heath and Hedy Zeer for their help in data collection and
   my colleague in the Anthropology Department, University of Calgary, S. Graham S.
   Watson, who has discussed this paper with me.

1. Fifty percent of Christian Arabs (N=20) and 37% of Moslem Arabs (N=49) had
   shortwave radio sets. Discrepancies in N for different items of information are due
   to the fact that some respondents did not answer all the questions.
   Arab Stations Which can be Picked up on the Prairies by Shortwave Radios:
   I. Cairo (Egypt)
   1.Special North American program in Arabic everyday 6:45-7:45 P.M. (MST)
   2.Local daily programs for Egypt which can be picked up about eight months
   during the year (especially in the springtime). The reception in this case is not
   always clear.
   II. Beirut (Lebanon)
   Only local daily programs for Lebanon which can be picked up with difficulty.
   III. Algiers (Algeria)
   Same as in II.
   IV. Baghdad (Iraq)
   Same as in II and III.
   V. B.B.C. (London), Voice of America (Washington, D.C.) and Moscow (U.S.S.R.)
   also have regular Arabic programs (news, music, etc.) that can be picked up on the
   Prairies.
2. For a correct interpretation of the data in Table III it should be noted that the question
   asked was about the news of the Arab-Israeli war in the Middle East. The position of
   the Moslem Arabs is very clear on this issue, and it probably influenced their
   responses to the question.
3. In research studies for the Special Senate Committee on Mass Media it is reported that
   in Canada 83% of those over fifteen years of age listen to radio daily. The number of
   hours is not reported. (Report of the Special Senate Committee on Mass Media,
   1970:III, 11).
4. In the research studies for the Special Committee on Mass Media it is reported that
   96% of Canadians have at least one T.V. set in their homes. *Ibid.*, p. 11.
5. Comparable data for Christians were not obtained. In the research studies for the
   Special Senate Committee on Mass Media it is reported that in Canada 87% of
   homes receive daily newspapers. *Ibid*, p. 12.
6. It may be reasonably argued that the differences between Moslem Arab and Christian
   Arab immigrants is due to the differences in their socioeconomic standings. This
   may be true. However, the intention of the study is exploratory. Its aim is to identify
   the possible consequences of access to foreign broadcasts from abroad by an ethnic
   immigrant community. The small community of Moslem Arab immigrants in the
   Canadian Prairie City seems to serve this purpose very well.
7. Lasswell does not include entertainment in his structural functional scheme of
   communication (Lasswell, 1948).
8. Although the organizing framework of Wright's and consequently this paper's is based
   on functional analysis, limitation of space does not allow any discussion of this
   subject. For a discussion on functional analysis in sociology see Merton, 1957:
   1984.

9. For the support of this point see Table II (First row of the Table).
10. See Table II (Second and fourth row of the Table), and Table III.
11. See Table II (First row of the Table).
12. See Table III (Last row of the Table).
13. See Table III (Last row of the Table).
14. See Table VIII (Last two rows of the Table).
15. See Table II (Second row of the Table).
16. See Table V.
17. See Table V (Third row of the Table).
18. See Table V.
19. See Table II (First row of the Table) and Table V.
20. See Tables IX and II (First and fifth rows of the Table).
21. See Table VIII (Last two rows of the Table).
22. See Tables II and V.
23. See Tables I, IV and VI (Third row of the Table).
24. See Tables XIII and XIV.
25. See Tables I, IV, V and VI.
26. See Tables X and XI.
27. See Tables VII and XII.
28. Compare Table I with Table XIII, and Table IV with Table XIV.
29. Although news appear to be the most popular Canadian radio program among Moslem Arab immigrants (Table XIV), from Tables XIII, XV, and XVI one can make the logical inference that their exposure to the Canadian electronic media, except for T.V., is very limited and consequently their exposure to the news from these media subnormal. Note that there are only three persons among Moslem Arabs who receive daily newspapers regularly.
30 See Table XVI.
31. Ibid.
32. See Tables XIII, XIV, and XVII, and note also that there are only three persons who receive daily newspaper regularly among Moslem Arab immigrants.
33. Some of the functions and dysfunctions presented in Charts I and II have also been discussed by Wright in his scheme (i.e., opinion leadership, warning and instrumental functions, cultural growth, and continuation of socialization among adults). Giving reference for each item separately would have been rather cumbersome. Thus the present paper is indebted to Wright not only for its organizing scheme, but also for some of its contents (Wright, 1960).
34. The exploitation of modern technology for the purpose of preservation of tradition values has a wide range of applications. For instance, Srinivas reports that the introduction of the printing press in India made possible the transmission of not only modern knowledge, but also knowledge of traditional epics, mythology, lives of saints, and other religious literature (Srinivas, 1969:55). Plotnicov also reports a similar situation in Nigeria where the traditional social institutions have been preserved in urban settings with the assistance of modern technology (Plotnicov, 1970).

# REFERENCES

Bell, Daniel. 1961. *The End of Ideology*. New York: Collier Books.

Blumer, Herbert. 1946. "Collective Behavior," pp. 170-222 in Alfred M. Lee (ed.), *Principles of Sociology*. New York: Barnes and Noble.

Coser, Lewis A. 1960. "Comments on Bauer and Bauer's America, Mass Society and Mass Media." *Journal of Social Issues* 16:78-84.

Friedson, Eliot. 1953. "Communication Research and the Concepts of Mass." *American Sociological Review*, 18:313-317.

Josephson, Eric and Mary Josephson (eds.). 1962. *Man Alone*. New York: Dell Publishing Co.

Kaplan, Abraham. 1967. "The Aesthetics of the Popular Arts," in J.R. Hall and B. Vlanov (eds.), *Modern Culture and The Arts*. New York: McGraw-Hill.

Katz, Elihu and Paul Lazarsfeld. 1955. *Personal Influence*. Glencoe: The Free Press

Klapp, Orrin E. 1969. *Collective Search for Identity*. New York: Holt, Rinehart and Winston.

Lasswell, Harold D. 1948. "The Structure and Function of Communication in Society," pp. 32-51 in L. Bryson (ed.), *The Communication of Ideas*, New York: Harper.

Lazarsfeld, Paul and Robert K. Merton. 1948. "Mass Communication, Popular Taste and Organized Social Action," pp. 95-118 in L. Bryson (ed.), *The Communication of Ideas*. New York: Harper.

Lowenthal, Leo. 1950. "Historical Perspectives of Popular Culture," *American Journal of Sociology*, 55:323-332.

MacDonald, Dwight. 1962. *Against the American Grain*. New York: Random House.

Merton, Robert K. 1957. *Social Theory and Social Structure*. Glencoe: The Free Press

Mills, C. Wright. 1959. *The Power Elite*. New York: Oxford University Press.

Plotnicov, Leonard. 1970. "The Persistence of Traditional Social Institutions," pp. 66-82, in Peter C. W. Gutkin (ed.), *The Passing of Tribal Man in Africa*. Leiden, The Netherlands: E. J. Brill.

Porter, John. 1967. *The Vertical Mosaic: An Analysis of Social Class and Power in Canada*. Toronto: University of Toronto Press.

Rosenberg, Bernard. 1957. "Mass Culture in America," pp. 3-12 in Bernard Rosenberg and David Manning White (eds.), *Mass Culture: The Popular Arts in America*. New York: The Free Press.

Srinivas, M. N.. 1969. *Social Change in India*. Los Angeles, California: University of California Press.

Vidich, Arthur J. and Joseph Bensman. 1960. *Small Town in Mass Society*. New York: Doubleday & Co.

Wright, Charles R. 1960. "Functional Analysis and Mass Communications, *Public Opinion Quarterly*, 24:605-620. 1970. *Report of the Special Senate Committee on Mass Media*, Volume III. Ottawa: Queen's Printer for Canada.

# GROUP INFLUENCE, MASS MEDIA AND MUSICAL TASTE AMONG CANADIAN STUDENTS*

*Relatives most important factor for high culture listeners while radio most important for mass culture listeners.*

Research evidence clearly shows that both interpersonal relations and social characteristics of the audience are important variables in understanding patterns of media usage.[1] However, most of these studies are based on data from the United States. Cross-cultural and comparative studies not only help broaden the base of our generalizations, but also produce a sharper picture by the introduction of new variables. This study, therefore, deals with group influences in the acquisition of musical taste as well as the social characteristics associated with various musical tastes among Canadian male university students.

## METHOD

Data on musical interests of 216 full-time, third year, male students at a university in western Canada, in five different areas of study were obtained via telephone interviews during March 1971.[2] The five areas of study were: social science (history and political science majors), science (chemistry, physics and geology majors), business, engineering, and English and philosophy.[3]

Two types of music were distinguished — high culture music and mass culture music. High culture music:

1) is created by or under the supervision of a cultural elite operating within some aesthetic, literary or scientific tradition. . .

2) critical standards independent of the consumer of the product are systematically applied to it. . .[4]

High culture music refers to music which is usually considered "serious" or "classical." Mass culture music referred to those musical product

. . .manufactured solely for a mass market. Associated characteristics, not intrinsic to the definition, are standardization of product and mass behavior in its use. . .[5]

Operationally, high culture music was defined as any reported composition written by a composer listed in the chronology of musicians in *Listener's Guide to Musical Understanding*.[6] Mass culture music was defined as any reported composer or music by a composer not listed in the *Guide*.

Respondents were then classified as one of three types of listeners, depending upon the frequency with which they reported listening to various types of recorded music. A high culture listener was one who listened to high culture music frequently, even though he may have also listened to mass culture music. One who listened to mass culture music and occasionally to high culture music was classified as a mixed listener. A mass culture listener was one whose listening was devoted entirely to mass culture music.

The respondent also was asked to indicate the source of initial interest in listening to a particular type of music, the person(s) with whom he listened to his preferred type of music, the person(s) with whom he discussed music and how frequently, the musical taste of his friends, and family members who currently played a musical instrument.

Finally, along with some demographic attributes of the respondents, questions were also asked regarding their generation Canadian, their religious preference and their degree of religiosity.

# FINDINGS

*Group Influence.* How one acquires musical taste is probably a complex process extending over a number of years and is beyond the scope of this exploratory study. Also important is that one's current taste may not be the same as it was in the past or what it will be in the future. This section is concerned only with the presence of group influence and the possible relation between certain types of influence and certain types of musical taste.

Table 1 shows that relatives appear to be of greatest importance for the introduction of high culture listeners to music.[7] Attending live performance and playing an instrument follow. Personal choice, friends, a combination of friends and radio are of less importance. Radio is the least important of all.

For mixed listeners, playing an instrument was reported of greater importance as an initial source of interest in music than attending live performance, followed by personal choice, a combination of friends and radio, radio and friends. The least significant are relatives.

The largest percentage among the mass culture listeners indicated that their current taste in music was acquired directly from radio. Friends, a combination of friends and radio, personal choice, relatives and playing an instrument follow in that order. The least important factor is attending live performance.

Table 2, showing interpersonal relations, indicates that high culture listeners tend to listen to music alone while mass culture listeners tend to listen often with other people. Mixed listeners are in between.

## Group Influence, Mass Media and Musical Taste

In discussing music, it appears that high culture listeners are more likely to discuss music with relatives. However, mixed culture listeners are more likely to discuss music with friends and relatives, and mass culture listeners with friends only. When asked about the frequency of discussion, it was discovered that mass culture listeners were most likely to talk about music at least once a week (46%), followed by mixed (33%), then by high culture listeners (28%).

As for the musical taste of respondents' friends, mass culture listeners were more likely to cite friends as having the same taste in music, followed by mixed, then by high culture listeners.

TABLE 1

Type of Listener by Reported Sources of Initial Interest in Music, in Percent

Type of Listener

| Source of Initial Interest | High Culture | Mixed | Mass Culture | (N) |
|---|---|---|---|---|
| Personal Influence | | | | |
| Friends | 12 | 22 | 66 | (32) |
| Relatives | 41 | 9 | 50 | (32) |
| Personal Influence & Radio | | | | |
| Friends & Radio | 11 | 25 | 64 | (28) |
| Relatives & Radio | 0 | 25 | 75 | (4) |
| Radio Only | 3 | 23 | 74 | (65) |
| Other Sources | | | | |
| Attending Live Performance | 33.3 | 33.3 | 33.3 | (12) |
| Playing an Instrument | 18 | 46 | 36 | (11) |
| Own Personal Choice | 17 | 31 | 52 | (23) |
| Ambiguous | 40 | 40 | 20 | (5) |
| Don't Know | 0 | 0 | 100 | (4) |

Respondents were also asked to list family members who currently played a musical instrument. Responses to this question indicate that high culture listeners are more likely to come from homes where two or more family members play a musical instrument than mixed or mass culture listeners. Mass and mixed culture listeners are more likely than high culture listeners to come from homes where no one plays an instrument.

*Social Characteristics.* According to Wilensky, generation, major area of study, religious preference and strength of religious feelings were considered important variables in understanding the various types of listeners.[8]

The data on generation Canadian in Table 3 indicate that first and second generation show a higher proportion among high culture listeners than among mixed or mass culture listeners.

With respect to major area of study, Table 3 indicates that the largest proportion of high culture listeners are among English and philosophy majors. Science majors are next, followed by social science majors, engineering and business students. The same rank order is true for the mixed culture listeners, except that business and engineering students change places here. With respect to mass culture listeners, the rank order is in the opposite direction.

TABLE 2

Type of Listener by Interpersonal Relations, in Percent

Type of Listener

| Interpersonal Relations | High Culture | Mixed | Mass Culture | (N) |
|---|---|---|---|---|
| With Whom One Listens* | | | | |
| Alone | 21 | 25 | 54 | (81) |
| Alone and With Others | 19 | 19 | 62 | (59) |
| Mostly with Others | 8 | 26 | 66 | (76) |
| With Whom Music is Discussed** | | | | |
| No One | 9 | 27 | 64 | (55) |
| With Friends | 12 | 20 | 68 | (113) |
| With Relatives | 40 | 13 | 47 | (15) |
| With Friends & Relatives | 30 | 34 | 36 | (33) |
| Musical Taste of Friends*** | | | | |
| Similar | 14 | 22 | 64 | (145) |
| Different | 20 | 27 | 53 | (66) |
| Don't Know | 20 | 20 | 60 | (5) |

*$X^2 = 6.2$, 4 df, p = .20
**$X^2 = 15.8$, 6 df, p = .02
***$X^2 = 2.1$, 2 df, p = .20

Analysis of religious preference shows that Catholics tend to show a higher concentration among high culture listeners.[9] The data for mixed listeners also show a higher concentration of Catholics among this group. Students with no religious preference and those of Protestant faith are dominant among the mass culture listeners.

The frequency with which church is attended is taken as an index of strength of religious feeling. It appears that high and mixed culture listeners have a stronger religious feeling than mass culture listeners.

TABLE 3

Type of Listener by Various Social Characteristics, in Percent

| Social Characteristics | High Culture | Mixed | Mass Culture | (N) |
|---|---|---|---|---|
| Generation Canadian* | | | | |
| First and second | 23 | 22 | 55 | (74) |
| Third and more | 12 | 25 | 63 | (142) |
| | | | | |
| Major Area of Study** | | | | |
| English and Philosophy | 27 | 37 | 36 | (41) |
| Science | 20 | 25 | 55 | (40) |
| Social Science | 13 | 24 | 63 | (62) |
| Business | 8 | 22 | 70 | (37) |
| Engineering | 11 | 8 | 81 | (36) |
| | | | | |
| Religious Preference*** | | | | |
| Catholic | 23 | 26 | 51 | (35) |
| Protestant | 17 | 23 | 60 | (91) |
| Other | 17 | 33 | 50 | (6) |
| None | 12 | 23 | 65 | (84) |
| | | | | |
| Church Attendance**** | | | | |
| Less than once a month | 14 | 22 | 64 | (176) |
| Once a month or more | 25 | 30 | 45 | (40) |

*$X^2 = 4.42$, 2 df, p = .20
**$X^2 = 15.51$, 8 df, p = .05
***$X^2 = 2.06$, 6 df, n.s.
****$X^2 = 5.60$, 2 df, p = .10

# DISCUSSION

With respect to group influence in the acquisition of musical taste the data in Table 1 suggest that relatives in the case of high culture listeners have influence. After radio, friends are influential among mass culture listeners.

However, group influence may also occur in subtle forms in a variety of interpersonal relations. The data in Table 2 seem to corroborate those in Table 1 with respect to the influence of relatives and friends for the high culture and mass culture listeners respectively. The data for mixed listeners, probably because of their middle position between the two other groups, do not show consistency.

As for the social characteristics associated with each type of listener, it seems that European orientation -- either by being first and second generation Canadian or by studying academic subjects with high European content such as English and philosophy -- is responsible for high culture preference in music (Table 3).[10]

Religious preference and strength of religious feeling appear to be related to type of listening in the sense that the percentage of Catholics among high and mixed culture listeners is higher, and high and mixed culture listeners attend church more frequently (Table 3). However, when generation is held constant, high culture listeners are most likely to express no religious preference, followed by mixed, then by mass culture listeners. Again, little difference is found in the proportion of Protestants or Catholics among the three types of listeners. In other words, the findings in Table 3 regarding religion appear to be a byproduct of the tendency of first and second generation to be both high culture listeners and Catholic.

The present study has limitations. Firstly, due to the nature of our sample the findings of this study should be regarded as only suggestive. Secondly, to the people involved with music it is apparent that the definition of mass culture in the present study is broad and crude in that it includes in one category rock, folk, jazz, ethnic, and country and western music. Yet these types of music are not categorically the same. For instance, jazz differs in its complexity and structure from other types of music. However, in an exploratory study with limited resources, it makes some sense to simply dichotomize high culture and nonhigh culture music.

# NOTES

* Reprinted from *Journalism Quarterly*, Vol. 51, No. 4, (Winter 1974) pp. 705-709. Co-authored by Carole L. Heath.
1. The influence of social relationships among audiences in understanding what songs become popular and reaction toward songs has been described by David Riesman,

## Group Influence, Mass Media and Musical Taste

"Listening to Popular Music," *American Quarterly*, 2:259-72 (Fall 1950); and Nicholas Tucker, *Understanding the Mass Media* (Cambridge: The University Press, 1966). Parental influence has also received attention by Steven H. Chafee, Jack M. McLeod and Charles K. Atkin, "Parental Influence & Adolescent Media Use," *American Behavioral Scientist*, 4:323-39 (January-February 1971); and Scott Ward and Daniel Wackman, "Family and Media Influence on Adolescent Consumer Learning," *Ibid.*, pp. 415-27. Also in the same issue see Roger L. Brown and Michael O'Leary, "Pop Music in an English Secondary School," pp. 401-13, which examines pop music as a source of prestige among peer groups. Actually the whole issue of this source is devoted to the studies on mass communication and youth, most of which are at least tangentially relevant to the present paper. For another study on the influence of the peer group see John Johnstone and Elihu Katz, "Youth and Popular Music: A Study in the Sociology of Taste," *American Journal of Sociology*, 62:563-8 (May 1957). Taste in music has been found to be correlated with educational level and metropolitan living by Paul F. Lazarsfeld, *The People Look at Radio* (Chapel Hill: University of North Carolina Press, 1946). The same taste has been found related to occupation, age and sex by Karl Schuessler, "Social Background and Musical Taste," *American Sociological Review*, 18: 330-5 (June 1948). Peterson has found age, race, social class and religiosity correlated with musical taste in Richard A. Peterson, "The Manufacture of Culture: The Case of Popular Music," a paper presented to the American Sociological Association (1970). Finally in a comprehensive study high culture use in books, radio, television and magazine was predicted from the amount of exposure to liberal arts education in university, religious preference and generation American by Harold L. Wilensky, "Mass Society and Mass Culture," *American Sociological Review*, 29: 173-97 (April 1964). In the choice of some variables the present study has been influenced by Wilensky.

2. Because the study was designed to examine the relationship between certain variables and the type of musical taste, stratified random sampling was used. From a list of all full-time, third-year male students, 40 or more respondents were selected randomly for each area of study. The rationale behind the selection of full-time, third-year students was the fact that one of our variables was major area of study. Female students were excluded to control for sex in the analysis. The interviewers were six female sociology graduate students. Telephone contacts proved more convenient during the pre-testing of the questionnaire. On the average each interview lasted about 15 minutes. There were no refusals. Fourteen respondents who said that they did not listen to any music or records were excluded.

3. Wilensky reports that a strong liberal arts education was associated with a "high brow" media exposure and engineers were more attracted to the "low brow" materials. See Wilensky, *op cit.* We have differentiated between science, social science, and English and philosophy in order to distinguish the influence of the different parts of a liberal arts education. Business has been added for its similarity with engineering in that both fields are in applied areas with an emphasis on practicality.

4. Wilensky, *op. cit.*, pp. 175-6.

6. Leon Dallin, *Listener's Guide to Musical Understanding* (Dubuque: William C. Brown Company, 1959).

7. Only rows with N>10 are considered in the analysis of data from Table 1. Considering only personal influence, $X^2$ (between rows one and two in the table) = 5.08, 2 df, p. = .10. Comparing personal influence (rows one and two combined) personal

influence and radio (rows three and four combined), and radio only (row five)X2 = 17.18, 4df, p = .01.
8. Wilensky, *op. cit.*
9. The category "Other religious preference" has been ignored because of small N.
10. It is interesting to note that 76% of the English and philosophy students and only 26% of science students are third or more generation Canadians from Europe. The same data for social science, engineering and business students are 58%, 60% and 65% respectively.

# SECTION III

# NEWS DIFFUSION STUDIES

# DIFFUSION OF A SAD NEWS EVENT IN A CANADIAN CITY*

*ABSTRACT: This study describes the various aspects of the diffusion of sad news in a Canadian setting. The findings are also compared with those of American diffusion studies and the points of agreement and disagreement are discussed.*

On Sunday, March 5, 1967, at 9:20 a.m. (MST) Georges Vanier, Governor General of Canada died at his official residence in Ottawa. Governor General Vanier took office on September 15, 1959. Because of his central role in many governmental ceremonies, and because of his official visits as the representative of the Queen to many parts of the country, Georges Vanier was a well-known figure throughout Canada at the time of his death.

The purpose of this paper is to examine through what channels people first learned about this event, how long it took for the news to get around, what sources were consulted for additional information, and how much interpersonal communication was resulted. This is a report on a study which closely parallels two American studies.[1] However, the data came from a Canadian setting.

## METHOD

Two populations were selected as subjects. First, two random samples of fifty male and fifty female undergraduates in the Faculty of Arts and Science at The University of Calgary, who were already selected for another study, were interviewed between March 8 and 11. Data from forty-four male and forty-eight female students were collected.

The second population consisted of the adult residents in a working-class community in Calgary. The residents of every third house in the community were contacted independently in the evening of March 7, and a total of 130 interviews were completed. Table I** shows some demographic characteristics of these two populations.

---

** Tables are at the end of the chapter.

# RESULTS

*How many people knew of Governor General Vanier's death?* All the members of the University samples knew of the news. In the working-class community ninety-seven percent males and ninety-nine percent females knew of the news.

*How did the knowers become knowers?* Through what channels did they first learn the news? Table II shows the proportion of persons of each population learning of the Governor General's death from various media. The following patterns may be noted:

1. The dominant role of the radio in both populations.
2. The relative importance of the interpersonal communication, except for the male university students.
3. The importance of T.V. in the laboring community, except for the male university students.[2]

Radio seems to be the most important source of the news. Not only is radio most important for both populations in general, but it is the most important initial source for all subgroups within those populations. While the overall difference between the university students and the laboring community is statistically significant (P < .05), other differences between the subgroups within each population are not.

After radio comes interpersonal communication in initially informing both populations. Although more people in the laboring community were thus informed, the difference between the two populations is not statistically significant. As for the differences between the subgroups within each population, only the difference between the male and female students is significant (P < .001).

After radio and interpersonal communication comes T.V. which seems to have a more dominant role in the laboring community as the initial source of information than among the university students. However, the difference is not statistically significant.

The first newspaper reporting the death of the Governor General was available to the public at 7:00 a.m., Monday, March 6. This fact should explain the minor role of the newspaper as the initial source of the news.

*When did they learn the news?* The first news of Governor General Vanier's death was made available in Calgary at 10:10 a.m. (MST). The median hour of learning for the two populations and the subgroups is shown in Table III. Thus it seems that the university students heard the news earlier than the laboring community, and the females in both populations heard the news earlier than the males.

There are also time differences within each population with respect to the medium through which the first information was provided. As Table IV shows people who heard the news from other persons learned sooner than those learning by other means in the working-class community. Among the students the median time of learning is the same for radio and interpersonal medium. Those who obtained their first information about the event from T.V. learned considerably later.

*What were the supplementary sources of information?* To what extent did these populations consult additional sources of information in an effort to verify or supplement their knowledge of this event? Table V shows the proportion of knowers in each population who, upon hearing of Governor General Vanier's death, consulted the various media for gaining additional information or interpretation of the news event.

Comparing the two populations in Table V we find that, considering all media, university students were more concerned about the news than the working-class community; that women in both populations were more concerned than men, especially in the working-class community. But neither of these differences are statistically significant.

For the knowers who did seek additional information, radio appears to be the preferred supplementary source of information in both populations. But while for the university students the next most preferred source was the newspaper, for the working-class community it was T.V. Other persons as an additional source of information are sought more frequently by the university students than by the laboring community. As for the subgroups within each population, women tend to rely more heavily on radio as a supplementary source of information than men in both populations, and among the university students males rely more on the newspaper than females. None of the above differences are statistically significant.

*Where did they learn the news?* Tables VI to IX report the importance of location at the time of the first media exposure for the two populations. As Tables VI and VII show, all media of communication were more active at private homes than at any other place. We also find that radio informed almost all the people who were in their cars at the time of the first exposure. Interpersonal channel was the dominant initial source of the news for those who were at public places, both among the university students and working-class community. It was also the dominant source for persons at work and those who were visiting relatives and friends among the working-class community.

According to Table VIII there seems to be a tendency among people in private homes to learn the news earlier than those in other locations.

# Canadian Studies in Mass Communication

Table IX shows that while among the university students there is almost no difference between percentages of males and females who heard the news at home, among the working-class community there is a significant difference (P < .002). It is also found that there are more males than females who have heard the news in the car for both groups. However, more females from the University and more males from the working-class community heard the news in public places.

*The interpersonal communication.* Three aspects of the interpersonal communication will be considered here: (1) the social structure of initial diffusion, (2) the amount of conversation generated by the news event, and (3) the number of new knowers informed from that conversation.

1. *Social structure of initial diffusion.* We have already noted in Table II that interpersonal communication accounted for twenty-seven percent of the initial learning in the working-class community and twenty-one percent among the university students. When the respondents indicated they had learned the news from an interpersonal source, they were asked to specify their general social relationship to that source. The data in Table X suggest the importance of the primary group relationships, especially the family, for both populations. However, the fact that the news event had occurred on a holiday rather than on a work day probably has affected the results.

2. *Conversation about the news event.* We asked our subject if upon learning of the Governor General's death they had talked to anybody about it. In the working-class community 127 news knowers talked to 674 people about the news, while 92 university student news knowers talked to 478 people. In comparing the two groups it should be remembered that the difference in interview time gave the university students more opportunity for talking about the news. It may also be reported that in the working-class community twenty-six percent of the knowers said they talked to no one about the news, but only eleven percent of the university students did not engage in conversation.

While the majority of persons in both populations talked to someone about the news, each population contained few persons who can be described as talkative. Among the university students the most talkative male and female each talked to 22 persons about the news event. In the working-class community they talked to 35 and 20 persons respectively. On the whole in both populations females were found to be more talkative than males. This difference may be due to the fact that, on the average, men learned the news later than women in both populations. These differences are reported in table XI.

3. *New knowers informed.* To what extent did the conversation reported result in the diffusion of the news? In both populations about thirteen percent of the conversations on the Vanier story involved informing people of his death. The working-class community claimed they had informed 95 persons in their

conversations with 674 people, while the university students said they informed 64 in their talks with 478 persons. Thus it appears that conversation does not necessarily result in the diffusion of the news. Table XII gives a more complete picture of this pattern of communication.

# DISCUSSION

It is not the primary purpose of this paper to test any specific hypothesis on mass communication or the process of news diffusion, rather to present descriptive information concerning various aspects of diffusion of a news event in a Canadian city.

Comparing the present study with similar previous studies, there seems to be both points of agreement and disagreement. For instance, the findings of Larsen and Hill agree with those of the present study regarding the tendency among women and the more educated to learn the news earlier than men and the less educated; more people learning the news from mass media sources than through interpersonal communication; and radio being the single most important initial source of the news. However, the present study disagrees with Larsen and Hill's finding that males talked to more people about the news than did women. Again, according to Hill and Bonjean, interpersonal communication was the single most important source of initial learning and it was almost as rapid as was learning from other media sources. In the present study, it is found that while learning through interpersonal medium of communication was rapid, and sometimes even more rapid than learning from other media, interpersonal communication was not the single most important source of initial learning.

Undoubtedly, the news value and the time of an event, among various other factors, influence the pattern and the speed of diffusion. For instance, it is reasonable to assume that the announcement of Senator Taft's death as reported by Larsen and Hill,[3] had a different psychological impact than the news of President Kennedy's assassination studied by Hill and Bonjean[4] and others. Again, one is almost certain that the release of the news of these two events on Friday morning had encountered different kinds of routines of people than the announcement of Governor General Vanier's death on Sunday morning.

However, inspite of the differences in news value and release time, the consistency between the findings of the present study and Larsen and Hill study with respect to the tendency among women to hear the news before men and the more educated before the less educated seem to reject the hypothesis proposed by Hill and Bonjean which says, "that the speed of the diffusion process is a function of 'news value' of the event rather than the particular characteristics of the population being investigated."[5]

## Canadian Studies in Mass Communication

There is no question that the news value of an event influences its diffusion speed. But characteristics of the population also influences the pace of its diffusion. In other words, other things being equal, different segments of the population do not receive the news simultaneously no matter what the news value of an event.

TABLE I
CHARACTERISTICS OF THE TWO POPULATIONS

| | University Students | | | Working-Class Community | | |
|---|---|---|---|---|---|---|
| | Total | Male | Female | Total | Male | Female |
| Occupation | | | | | | |
| Professional and white collar | 71%** | | | 11%* | | |
| Skilled Manual | 26%** | | | 76%* | | |
| Unskilled manual | 03%** | | | 13%* | | |
| Median age | 20 | 20 | 19 | 37 | 37 | 36 |
| Mean no. of school years completed | | | | 9.22 | 8.9 | 9.5 |

*Housewives (N = 44); non-gainfully employed, and retired (N = 14) are not included.
** Occupation of parents is considered.

TABLE II
PROPORTION OF PERSONS LEARNING OF GOVERNOR GENERAL
VANIER'S DEATH FROM THE VARIOUS MEDIA

| Medium | University Students | | | Working-Class Community | | |
|---|---|---|---|---|---|---|
| | Total | Male | Female | Total | Male | Female |
| Radio | .68 | .68 | .69 | .53 | .49 | .57 |
| T.V. | .09 | .14 | .04 | .15 | .15 | .16 |
| Newspaper | .01 | .02 | - | .02 | .03 | .01 |
| Interpersonal | .21 | .14 | .27 | .27 | .30 | .25 |
| Did not know the source | .01 | .02 | - | - | - | - |
| Did not know of news | - | - | - | .02 | .03 | .01 |
| | N=92 | 44 | 48 | 130 | 61 | 69 |

TABLE III
MEDIAN HOUR OF LEARNING

| University* | | | |
|---|---|---|---|
| Males | 12:30 | p.m. | Sunday |
| Females | 2:00 | p.m. | Sunday |
| | 12:00 | noon | Sunday |
| Working-Class Community** | | | |
| Males | 3:00 | p.m. | Sunday |
| Females | 6:00 | p.m. | Sunday |
| | 2:30 | p.m. | Sunday |

\* Three persons did not know the time.
\*\*Two persons did not know the time.

TABLE IV
MEDIAN TIME OF LEARNING FOR PERSONS OBTAINING ORIGINAL
INFORMATION FROM THE VARIOUS MEDIA

| Medium | University Students | | Working-Class Community | |
|---|---|---|---|---|
| Radio | 12:00 Noon Sunday | (N=63) | 3:30 p.m. Sunday | (N=69) |
| T.V. | 5:15 p.m. Sunday | (N=8) | 6:00 p.m. Sunday | (N=20) |
| Newspaper | -- | (N=1) | -- | (N=2)** |
| Interpersonal | 12:00 Noon Sunday | (N=16)* | 2:30 p.m. Sunday | (N=34)*** |
| Did not know the source | -- | (N=1) | -- | -- |
| Did not know of news | -- | -- | -- | (N=3) |
| | | 89 | | 128 |

*Three persons did not know the time.
**One person did not know the time.
***One person did not know the time.

TABLE V
PROPORTION OF KNOWERS WHO CONSULTED THE VARIOUS MEDIA
FOR ADDITIONAL INFORMATION CONCERNING VANIER'S DEATH

| Medium Consulted | University Students | | | Working-Class Community | | |
|---|---|---|---|---|---|---|
| | Total | Male | Female | Total | Male | Female |
| Radio | .16 | .14 | .19 | .16 | .12 | .19 |
| T.V. | .03 | .02 | .04 | .13 | .12 | .13 |
| Newspaper | .13 | .16 | .10 | .08 | .09 | .09 |
| Other persons | .07 | .07 | .06 | .01 | .02 | - |
| 2 or more media | .09 | .07 | .10 | .05 | .03 | .07 |
| None | .52 | .55 | .51 | .57 | .62 | .52 |
| | N= 92 | 44 | 48 | 127* | 59 | 68 |

*Three persons did not know of news.

TABLE VI
PLACE AND SOURCE OF FIRST EXPOSURE (UNIVERSITY STUDENTS)

| Place of First Exposure | Source of First Exposure | | | | | | | | | |
|---|---|---|---|---|---|---|---|---|---|---|
| | Radio | | T.V. | | Interpersonal | | Newspaper | | Total | |
| | Number | Percent | Number | Percent | Number | Percent | Number | Percent | Number | Percent |
| At private home | 48 | 71 | 7 | 10 | 12 | 18 | 1 | 1 | 68 | 100 |
| At work | 2 | 100 | 0 | 0 | 0 | 0 | 0 | 0 | 2 | 100 |
| In car | 12 | 86 | 0 | 0 | 2 | 14 | 0 | 0 | 14 | 100 |
| At friends, relatives | 1 | 33 | 1 | 33 | 1 | 33 | 0 | 0 | 3 | 100 |
| Public places | 0 | 0 | 0 | 0 | 4 | 100 | 0 | 0 | 4 | 100 |
| D. K. | 0 | 0 | 0 | 0 | 0 | 0 | 0 | 0 | 0 | 0 |
| Total | 63 | 69 | 8 | 9 | 19 | 21 | 1 | 1 | 91* | 100 |

* One person did not know source of news.

TABLE VII
PLACE AND SOURCE OF FIRST EXPOSURE (WORKING-CLASS COMMUNITY)

| Place of First Exposure | Source of First Exposure | | | | | | | | Total | |
| --- | --- | --- | --- | --- | --- | --- | --- | --- | --- | --- |
| | Radio | | T.V. | | Interpersonal | | Newspaper | | | |
| | Number | Percent | Number | Percent | Number | Percent | Number | Percent | Number | Percent |
| At private home | 55 | 59 | 16 | 17 | 19 | 21 | 3 | 3 | 93 | 100 |
| At work | 3 | 33 | 1 | 11 | 5 | 56 | 0 | 0 | 9 | 100 |
| In car | 8 | 100 | 0 | 0 | 0 | 0 | 0 | 0 | 8 | 100 |
| At friends, relatives | 1 | 20 | 0 | 0 | 4 | 80 | 0 | 0 | 5 | 100 |
| Public places | 0 | 0 | 2 | 22 | 7 | 78 | 0 | 0 | 9 | 100 |
| D. K. | 2 | 67 | 1 | 33 | 0 | 0 | 0 | 0 | 3 | 100 |
| Total | 69 | 54 | 20 | 16 | 35 | 28 | 3 | 2 | 127* | 100 |

* three people did not know of news.

TABLE VIII
TIME AND PLACE OF FIRST EXPOSURE

| Time Elapsed Since News Released | University Students | | | | | | Working-Class Community | | | | | | TOTAL | |
| --- | --- | --- | --- | --- | --- | --- | --- | --- | --- | --- | --- | --- | --- | --- |
| | At private home | | Out of home | | Total | | At private home | | Out of home | | Total | | | |
| | No. | Percent | No. | Percent | No. | Percent | No. | Percent | No. | Percent | No. | Percent | No. | Percent |
| 15 minutes | 15 | 23 | 3 | 12 | 18 | 19 | 17 | 18 | 3 | 10 | 20 | 16 | 38 | 17 |
| 30 minutes | 0 | 0 | 0 | 0 | 0 | 0 | 1 | 1 | 0 | 0 | 1 | 1 | 1 | 1 |
| 45 minutes | 11 | 16 | 4 | 17 | 15 | 16 | 8 | 9 | 1 | 3 | 9 | 8 | 24 | 10 |
| 60 minutes | 0 | 0 | 1 | 4 | 1 | 1 | 2 | 2 | 4 | 13 | 6 | 5 | 7 | 3 |
| 90 minutes | 2 | 3 | 2 | 8 | 4 | 4 | 2 | 2 | 2 | 6 | 4 | 3 | 8 | 4 |
| 2 hours | 9 | 13 | 0 | 0 | 9 | 10 | 11 | 12 | 3 | 10 | 14 | 11 | 23 | 11 |
| 3 hours | 6 | 9 | 2 | 8 | 8 | 9 | 3 | 3 | 0 | 0 | 3 | 2 | 11 | 5 |
| 4-5 hours | 1 | 1 | 4 | 18 | 5 | 6 | 8 | 9 | 6 | 19 | 14 | 11 | 19 | 9 |
| 6 hours+ | 22 | 32 | 7 | 29 | 29 | 32 | 39 | 42 | 12 | 39 | 51 | 41 | 80 | 37 |
| D. K. | 2 | 3 | 1 | 4 | 3 | 3 | 2 | 2 | 0 | 0 | 2 | 2 | 5 | 3 |
| Total | 68 | 100 | 24 | 100 | 92 | 100 | 93 | 100 | 31 | 100 | 124* | 100 | 216 | 100 |

Place of First Exposure

*Three people did not know of news, and three people did not know place of first exposure.

TABLE IX
SEX AND PLACE OF FIRST EXPOSURE

| Place of First Exposure | Sex | | | | | | | | | | | | | TOTAL | |
| | University Students | | | | | | Working-Class Community | | | | | | | | |
| | Male | | Female | | Total | | Male | | Female | | Total | | | | |
| | No. | Percent | No. | Percent | No. | Percent | No. | Percent | No. | Percent | No. | Percent | | No. | Percent |
|---|---|---|---|---|---|---|---|---|---|---|---|---|---|---|---|
| At private home | 32 | 73 | 36 | 75 | 68 | 75 | 35 | 60 | 58 | 84 | 93 | 73 | | 161 | 74 |
| At work | 0 | 0 | 2 | 5 | 2 | 2 | 6 | 10 | 3 | 4 | 9 | 7 | | 11 | 5 |
| In car | 11 | 25 | 4 | 8 | 15 | 16 | 6 | 10 | 2 | 3 | 8 | 6 | | 23 | 11 |
| At friends, relatives | 0 | 0 | 3 | 6 | 3 | 3 | 3 | 6 | 2 | 3 | 5 | 4 | | 8 | 3 |
| Public places | 1 | 2 | 3 | 6 | 4 | 4 | 6 | 10 | 3 | 4 | 9 | 7 | | 13 | 6 |
| D. K. | 0 | 0 | 0 | 0 | 0 | 0 | 2 | 4 | 1 | 2 | 3 | 3 | | 3 | 1 |
| Total | 44 | 100 | 48 | 100 | 92 | 100 | 58 | 100 | 69 | 100 | 127* | 100 | | 219 | 100 |

*Three people did not know of news.

TABLE X
RELATIONSHIP OF INTERPERSONAL INFORMER TO RESPONDENT

| | University Students | | | Working-Class Community | | |
|---|---|---|---|---|---|---|
| | Total | Male | Female | Total | Male | Female |
| Spouse | .05 | .14 | - | .26 | .33 | .17 |
| Children | - | - | - | .05 | - | .12 |
| Parents | .37 | .43 | .33 | .09 | - | .17 |
| Siblings | .05 | .14 | - | - | - | - |
| Family (unspecified) | .11 | - | .18 | .17 | .28 | .06 |
| Relative (unspecified) | - | - | - | .09 | .11 | .06 |
| Friend | .26 | .14 | .33 | .14 | .06 | .24 |
| Co-worker | .05 | - | .08 | .11 | .16 | .06 |
| Stranger | .11 | .14 | .08 | .09 | .06 | .12 |
| N = | 19 | 7 | 12 | 35 | 18 | 17 |

TABLE XI
MEDIAN NUMBER OF PERSONS TALKED TO

| | |
|---|---|
| University Students | 4 |
| Males | 3 |
| Females | 4 |
| Working-Class Community | 3 |
| Males | 2 |
| Females | 3 |

TABLE XII
NUMBER OF CONVERSATIONS RESULTING IN NEW KNOWERS
DIVIDED BY TOTAL NUMBER OF CONVERSATIONS

| | |
|---|---|
| University Students | .13 |
| Males | .11 |
| Females | .16 |
| Working-Class Community | .14 |
| Males | .11 |
| Females | .18 |

# Canadian Studies in Mass Communication

# NOTES

\*    A paper presented at the Canadian Learned Societies Meeting in Toronto (June, 1969). I am grateful to Dr. Herbert S. Armstrong, then the President of the University of Calgary, and Dr. Donald L. Mills, Chairman of the Department of Sociology and Anthropoloby in the Spring 1967, whose interest and support enabled me to obtain the necessary funds for data collection from the University on a very short notice. I wish to thank my students in Research Methods course in 1967 who did the interviewing. A subsequent grant from The University of Calgary Research Grants Committee helped to complete the study. Mrs. Carole Heath has assisted in the analysis of the data.

1. This is a rather repeat study of the one by Otto N. Larsen and Richard J. Hill, "Mass Media and Interpersonal Communications in the Diffusion of a News Event," *American Sociological Review,* 19 (August, 1954), pp. 426-433. Some data also parallel those collected by Richard J. Hill and Charles M. Bonjean, "News Diffusion: A Test of the Regularity Hypothesis," *Jouralism Quarterly,* 41 (Summer, 1964), pp. 336-342. For other studies on the diffusion of the news in the United States, see Delbert C. Miller, "A Research Note on Mass Communication," *American Sociological Review,* 10 (October, 1945), pp. 691-694; Wayne Danielson, "Eisenhower's February Decision: A Study of News Impact," *Journalism Quarterly,* 33 (Fall, 1956), pp. 433-441; Paul Deutschmann and Wayne Danielson, "Diffusion of Knowledge of the Major News Story," *Journalism Quarterly,* 37 (Summer, 1960), pp. 345-355; Bradley S. Greenberg, "Diffusion of News of the Kennedy Assassination," *Public Opinion Quarterly,* 28 (Summer, 1964), pp. 225-232; and, Richard W. Budd, Malcolm S. MacLean, Jr., and Arthur M. Barnes, "Regularities in the Diffusion of Two Major News Events," *Journalism Quarterly,* 43 (Summer, 1966), pp. 221-230, among others. For similar studies in non-Western societies see Ibrahim Abu-Lughod, "The Mass Media and Egyptian Village Life," *Social Forces,* 42 (October, 1963), pp. 97-104; and, S.C. Dube, "Communication, Innovation, and Planned Change in India," in Daniel Lerner and Wilbur Schramm, *Communication and Change in Developing Countries* (Honolulu: East West Centre Press, 1967), pp. 129-167.

2. One may be tempted to attribute this behavior of male university students to the fact that popular Sunday sports programs were telecast in the city on March 5 by the two television networks at 10:30 a.m., 12:00 noon, and 2:30 p.m. However, our data do not support this point (see Table IV).

3. Larsen and Hill, *loc. cit.*

4. Hill and Bonjean, *loc. cit.*

5. *Ibid,* p. 338.

# DIFFUSION OF A "HAPPY" NEWS EVENT*

*Diffusion of news of marriage of Prime Minister Trudeau followed same gross pattern as reported in other studies. Television, however, played a less important role than usual.*

Most news diffusion studies deal with "bad" news such as the death of a political leader, or uninteresting news like Alaskan statehood.[1] "Happy" news has not been studied. Further, most news diffusion research has been limited to the United States. This study examines the pattern and process of diffusion in a Canadian city of the "happy" news of Prime Minister Trudeau's marriage.[2]

Pierre Elliott Trudeau, the 51-year-old bachelor prime minister of Canada, was secretly married to Margaret Sinclair, 22, in Vancouver, British Columbia, on Thursday evening, March 4, 1971. The first news bulletin in Calgary, Alberta, flashed at 9:50 p.m., M.S.T. According to the evening paper, *The Calgary Herald*, "The bombshell announcement took the entire country by surprise."

*Sample and Method.* On Friday, March 5, at 7 p.m., 21 sociology students from the University of Calgary started interviewing by telephone a sample of 250 persons randomly selected from the current telephone directory. Most of the interviewing was completed within 24 hours from the time of the news release. By 5 p.m. Sunday, 186 interviews were completed (74%). Of the 64 remaining, 9 persons refused, 3 persons did not know enough English, 20 either had moved or there was no listing for them. The rest did not answer after two callbacks.

Calgary is a city of more than 400,000, with two television stations, six radio stations, and one morning and one evening newspaper.

## FINDINGS

*Rate of diffusion.* The news of Mr. Trudeau's marriage spread through Calgary with great speed. As Table 1 indicates, about half of our respondents knew of the event within 15 minutes after the news release. Within one and a half hours, an additional 1/6 knew of the event.

This rapid diffusion was due mostly to TV, which reached two-thirds of its eventual first-exposure audience within 15 minutes. Interpersonal channels took 45 minutes and radio two hours to reach half of their respective audiences. Although all of those who received the news by TV had heard of the event on Thursday, word of mouth and radio continued to inform their audience even during the next day. Table 1 shows that radio and the newspaper were most active in the early morning hours, and interpersonal channels during the working hours and after. Very few received the news via newspapers, mostly because the news was released after the evening newspaper was out. Finally, of the entire sample only three women did not know of the news.

TABLE 1
Cumulative Percentage of "Knowers"
by Source of First Exposure

| Time Elapsed since news Release | Radio | T.V. | Newspaper | Source Interpersonal | Sample |
|---|---|---|---|---|---|
| 15 minutes | 36 | 68 | - | 45 | 49 |
| 45 minutes | 40 | 77 | - | 52 | 55 |
| 90 minutes | 48 | 93 | - | 64 | 67 |
| Thursday | 50 | 100 | - | 82 | 75 |
| 10 hours | 95 | — | 75 | 82 | 92 |
| Friday | 100 | — | 100 | 100 | 100 |
| N | (62) | (82) | (8) | (31) | (183) |

The significance of television as initial source apparently is due to the time of the news break. In the studies of events whose news was released in the morning, radio or the newspaper appears to dominate television.[3] In the studies of the news with tremendous psychological impact, such as the assassination of President Kennedy, word of mouth often appears to be the initial source for more than 50% of the people.[4]

The first column in Table 2 shows the proportion who came to know of the event on Thursday evening, among various subgroups.[5] There are more knowers among men than women, and among housewives than non-housewives. With respect to age and education the relationship appears to be curvilinear. In other words, there are more knowers among the younger and the older and among the low and high educational categories than among the middle-aged and the middle educational group. There is practically no difference between the Canadian born and immigrants, and no difference between those who heard the news at home and outside.

*Media used for checking and more information.* The respondents were asked if they had checked the news after hearing it for the first time. Only 14% of knowers had checked the news, and radio was the most favored medium for

TABLE 2
Results of Learning News by Various Subgroups

| | Thursday evening % who heard news | % Exposed to Various Sources | | | | % who informed someone else | % who talked to 4+ persons | % who learned about Mrs. Trudeau | (N) |
| | | Radio | TV | News-paper | Inter-personal | | | | |
|---|---|---|---|---|---|---|---|---|---|
| Total Sample | 75 | 33 | 44 | 4 | 17 | 36 | 59 | 35 | (183) |
| Men | 80 | 36 | 41 | 1 | 21 | 29 | 66 | 34 | (80) |
| Women | 72 | 31 | 46 | 7 | 13 | 42 | 53 | 37 | (103) |
| Housewives | 75 | 31 | 49 | 9 | 10 | 44 | 42 | 39 | (58) |
| Non-housewives | 69 | 33 | 42 | 4 | 18 | 40 | 69 | 36 | (45) |
| Age Under 30 | 78 | 22 | 49 | 4 | 23 | 43 | 73 | 29 | (49) |
| Age 30-49 | 72 | 41 | 39 | 3 | 16 | 30 | 57 | 38 | (79) |
| Age 50+ | 77 | 31 | 48 | 8 | 13 | 40 | 50 | 42 | (48) |
| Education 8 years or less | 82 | 32 | 55 | 0 | 9 | 46 | 32 | 14 | (22) |
| Education 9 - 12 | 72 | 34 | 50 | 4 | 12 | 37 | 57 | 33 | (101) |
| Education 13+ | 78 | 34 | 31 | 7 | 27 | 32 | 75 | 51 | (59) |
| Canadian Born | 75 | 39 | 40 | 2 | 21 | 33 | 65 | 39 | (123) |
| Immigrant | 77 | 29 | 54 | 9 | 7 | 46 | 49 | 29 | (56) |
| Place of Exposure | | | | | | | | | |
| At home | 77 | | | | | 43 | 59 | 36 | (149) |
| Out of home | 76 | | | | | 27 | 64 | 36 | (33) |

103

checking. When the respondents were separated according to the initial source, it was found that, of those who had heard the news by word of mouth more than one-third checked the news; by contrast, only about one of every nine who heard it first via mass media checked on it elsewhere. This suggests that interpersonal sources are considered less reliable than media. Such a high trust in mass media with respect to learning about news is completely the opposite of the findings regarding persuasion. Research studies on attitude change consistently demonstrate the efficacy of person to person contact and face to face communication at the expense of mass media.[6]

The respondents were also asked if they had tried to find out more about Trudeau's marriage. The largest proportion of the people who wanted more information, 19%, used the newspaper for this purpose. Eleven percent used TV and 13% radio for obtaining more information, but none used interpersonal sources. About 10% used more than one medium for the same purpose.

*Source and individual attributes.* Columns 2-5 in Table 2 report the relationship between various media as initial source and the demographic attributes of their audience. It appears that women more than men got the news by TV and the newspaper. More men than women were exposed to radio and interpersonal channels than women.

However, if housewives are separated from other females, the non-housewives are more like men. More non-housewives than housewives got the news by radio and word of mouth, and they were less exposed to TV and newspaper than the housewives.

The relationship between age and different media as the initial source of the news appears to be curvilinear. The old and the young tend to use TV and newspaper more, and radio less, than the middle-aged, but older citizens are less likely to rely on word of mouth for obtaining the news.

There are positive correlations between education and using radio, inter-personal channel and the newspaper for obtaining news, but education is negatively related to the most popular source, TV.

Canadian born residents rely more than immigrants on radio and interpersonal channels. The reverse is true of newspapers and television.

Overall, the more a person was socially isolated the less he was exposed to interpersonal channels and more to the newspaper as initial source. Thus, women less than men, housewives less than non-housewives, people 50 or more years old less than the younger persons, uneducated less than educated, and immigrants less than the Canadian born were exposed first via interpersonal channels. The opposite relationship exists between these social attributes and newspaper reading, except for education.

## Diffusion of a Happy News Event

*Source and place of first exposure.* Table 3 shows that male-female differences are due almost entirely to the tendency for men to be out of the home when they first heard the news. This table reinforces the earlier finding reported with respect to the differences between housewives and non-housewives in their initial exposure to various media. That is, the difference between men and women seems to come from different situations rather than their sexual identities.

### TABLE 3
#### Source By Place of First Exposure and Sex, in Percent

| Source | | | | Place | | | |
|---|---|---|---|---|---|---|---|
| | At Home | | | | Out of Home | | |
| | M | F | T | | M | F | T |
| Radio | 32 | 30 | 31 | | 45 | 46 | 46 |
| T.V. | 52 | 51 | 51 | | 14 | 18 | 15 |
| News | 0 | 8 | 5 | | 5 | 0 | 3 |
| Interpersonal | 16 | 11 | 13 | | 36 | 36 | 36 |
| N | (57) | (92) | (149) | | (22) | (11) | (33) |

According to Table 3, TV appears to be a home bound medium. Radio is more frequently used by those who heard the news while out of home. Interpersonal channels are second only to radio as an out-of-home source.

*Effects of the news.* After people learn about an important event they often inform others and talk about the event. Columns 6 and 7 in table 2 indicate there was more talking than informing. Women informed more than men, but men talked more to several people about the event than women. Housewives informed someone more than did non-housewives. However, non-housewives were more likely to talk to more than three persons.

The less the education of a person the more he informed others. With respect to talking, the more educated talked more to several people than the less educated.

Those who were out of home when they received the news tended to inform less than those who were at home, but they were more likely to talk about the event than the respondents who heard it at home.

Column 8 in Table 2 reports the amount of learning that took place among various categories of respondents. During the interview the respondents were asked to tell what they knew about Mr. Trudeau's wife. The percentages who knew four or more items of correct information about her such as name and age, appear in this column. As might be expected, women more than men, and housewives more than non-housewives had learned about Mrs. Trudeau. Older people also knew more about her. Education was positively correlated with learning. Immigrants learned less than the native born. There was no relationship between the place of exposure to the news and learning.

When comparing the amount of learning with the amount of talking with more than three persons for men and women, housewives and non-housewives, and younger and older respondents, there seems to be a negative correlation between learning and talking. These findings suggest that talking with more people is not necessarily related to gaining more information about the event.

*Assessment of Trudeau and its effects.* The respondents' opinion of Mr. Trudeau as a prime minister seems to be related to their behavior. During the interview they were asked, "In general, how do you think Mr. Trudeau is handling the affairs of Canada, as a Prime Minister?" The question was followed by three alternative responses, "very well," "not so bad," and "poorly."

In general Trudeau fans (N =58) came to know about his marriage half an hour sooner than others (N=120). Again, 84% of the former and 70% of the latter groups knew of the event on Thursday, or the first days of the news release. With respect to the initial source of the news interpersonal channels seemed to inform Trudeau fans more frequently (22%) than others (15%). Supporters of the prime minister engaged in checking the news more frequently (23%) than the rest of the sample (11%). Those who liked Trudeau had learned more bits of information about his wife (43%) than those who did not like him (33%). Finally the correlation between liking Trudeau and the amount of talking about his marriage was positive. Those who like him showed a stronger tendency to talk to four or more persons (96%) than those who did not care for him (83%).

# DISCUSSION

Deutschmann and Danielson[7] and later Hill and Bonjean,[8] after comparing several studies, concluded that diffusion process in the case of significant but unexpected events is regular and have come up with some generalizations. It is necessary to compare the findings of this study with their generalizations.

Deutschmann and Danielson first suggest that time of day, nature of story, and other factors do not seem to alter the gross pattern very much. A diffusion curve begins with a big spurt and then tapers off toward the "bedtime" in the first day. In the second day it jumps upward again and then with the near saturation of the field it flattens. The diffusion in the present study seems to follow the same gross pattern, and thus our data support the above generalization. This is an important finding because the nature of the news story in the present study is different from others which have been investigated so far.

There are other findings of Deutschmann and Danielson which are in accord with those of the present study. For instance: the use of the newspaper mainly as a supplementary source, the greater tendency among men to be informed by interpersonal channel, and newspaper receiving taking place primarily in the home.

However, their hypothesis that television plays a major role in delivering important news, though supported by the present study, does not find support from studies of the news stories with tremendous psychological impact, or events whose news released in the morning portion of the day.[9]

Hill and Bonjean's suggestion that the greater the news value of an event, the more important will be interpersonal communication in the process of diffusion does not seem to be supported by the Canadian data. If there is a correlation between the amount of interpersonal communication and the news value of an event, the news of the ailing Governor General Vanier's expected death should have been communicated less frequently by word of mouth than the news of the secret marriage of a 51-year-old controversial, bachelor prime minister.[10] However, the interpersonal channel accounts for 24% for Vanier and 17% for Trudeau stories. Apparently time of day is an important variable here. While Vanier's story was released at 10 a.m. , Trudeau's broke out at 9:50 p.m., M.S.T. It is suggested that for the events that occur near, or in the evening the electronic media do not leave much room for the interpersonal channels.[11]

Hill and Bonjean's hypothesis which states that the greater the news value of an event, the more rapid the diffusion process, gains support from the Canadian data. The news of the Governor General Vanier's death spread less rapidly than Trudeau's marriage.[12]

Finally, social psychological variables except for some incidental references in the literature have seldom been directly investigated in diffusion studies.[13] Banta reports that Democrats more than the Republicans tended to disbelieve President Kennedy's assassination.[14] Sheatsley and Feldman make a passing reference to the amount of history learning which took place among those who were exposed to the mass media after the late President's violent death.[15]

The present study has demonstrated the value of social psychological variables in explaining the diffusion pattern and the impact of a news story by directly examining the popularity of the prime minister and the information about his wife which were learned by the respondents.

## Canadian Studies in Mass Communication

# NOTES

* Reprinted from *Journalism Quarterly*, Vol. 50, No. 2, Summer 1973, pp. 271-277.
   The author is associate professor sociology at the University of Calgary. He wishes to thank Dr. Robert W. Wright, dean of the Arts and Science Faculty, and Dr. Nancy E. Henderson, chairman of the Research Grants Committee at the University of Calgary, whose support made funds available for data collection and partial analysis. He also wishes to thank Carole Heath, Gunter Baureiss, Margot Jungling and Myron Story, graduate research assistants in the Department of Sociology, for their help.

1. For examples of death of a political leader stories see Delbert C. Miller, "A Research Note on Mass Communication," *American Sociological Review*, 10:691-4 (October 1945); Otto N. Larsen and Richard J. Hill, "Mass Media and Interpersonal Communication in the Diffusion of a News Event," *American Sociological Review*, 19:426-33 (August 1954); and Richard J. Hill and Charles M. Bonjean, "News Diffusion: A Test of Regularity Hypothesis," *Journalism Quarterly*, 41:336-42 (Summer 1964). For Alaskan story see Paul J. Deutschmann and Wayne A. Danielson, "Diffusion of Knowledge of the Major News Story," *Journalism Quarterly*, 37:345-55 (Summer 1960).

2. The only other Canadian study is about the diffusion of the news of the death of Georges Vanier, the Canadian Governor General, March 5, 1967, which is reported in a paper by Asghar Fathi, "Diffusion of a News Event in a Canadian City," presented at the annual meetings of the Canadian Sociology and Anthropology Association in Toronto, Ontario, June 1969.

3. For news stories released in the morning see Wayne A. Danielson, "Eisenhower's February Decision: A Study of News Impact," *Journalism Quarterly*, 33:433-41 (Fall 1956); M. Timothy O'Keefe, "The First Heart Transplant: A Study of Diffusion Among Doctors," *Journalism Quarterly*, 46:237-42 (Summer 1969); John B. Adams, James J. Muller, and Harold M. Wilson, "Diffusion of a 'Minor' Foreign Affairs News Event," *Journalism Quarterly*, 46:45-51 (Autumn 1969); Larsen and Hill, *op. cit.*, and Fathi, *op. cit.*

4. For news stories with tremendous psychological impact see Miller, *op. cit.*, Hill and Bonjean, *op. cit.*, and Stephen P. Spitzer, "Mass Media vs. Personal Sources of Information about the Presidential Assassination: A Comparison of Six Investigations," *Journal of Broadcasting*, 9:45-50 (Winter 1965).

5. Discrepancies in N in Tables 2 and 3 are due to the fact that some respondents did not answer all the questions.

6. See Elihu Katz and Paul F. Lazarsfeld, *Personal Influence: The Part Played by People in the Flow of Mass Communications* (Glencoe, Ill.: The Free Press, 1955); and Joseph T. Klapper, *The Effects of Mass Communication* (Glencoe, Ill.: The Free Press, 1960), pp. 62-97.

7. Deutschmann and Danielson, *op. cit.*

8. Hill and Bonjean, *op. cit.*

9. See footnotes 3 and 4 above.

10. If we take the speed of diffusion as our measure of news value, it took over three hours for the news of Vanier's death to reach 50% of the sample, whereas for Trudeau story it took only 15 minutes to reach half of the sample.

11. Allen and Colfax's study of the diffusion of President Johnson's unexpected announcement not to seek a second term, broadcast at 9:45 p.m. Sunday, March 31,

1968, in which the investigators discovered that only 5% of the knowers had heard the news by word of mouth, supports the same hypothesis. See Irving L. Allen and J. David Colfax, "The Diffusion of News of LBJ's March 31 Decision," *Journalism Quarterly*, 46:321-4 (Summer 1968).

Although Greenberg has shown that for the events which go unnoticed by the majority the interpersonal sources will also be high, his curvilinear hypothesis is not applicable to the Canadian data because the percentage of awareness is about 98% in both Trudeau and Vanier stories. See Bradley S. Greenberg, "Person to Person Communication in the Diffusion of News Events," *Journalism Quarterly*, 41:489-94 (Autumn 1964).

12. See footnote 10 above.

13. Two exceptions come to mind: first, Greenberg who makes a distinction between "importance" and "attention" given to a news event; and second, Adams *et al.*, who investigate the difference between the Catholic and non-Catholic subjects in the study of the news of Pope Paul's encyclical. See Greenberg, *op. cit.*, and Adams, Mullen, and Wilson, *op. cit.*

   For a criticism of diffusion studies because of their lack of social-psychological variables see Verling C. Troldahl, "Studies of Consumption of Mass Media Content," *Journalism Quarterly*, 42:602 (Autumn 1965).

14. Thomas J. Banta, "The Kennedy Assassination: Early Thoughts and Emotions," *Public Opinion Quarterly*, 28:216-24 (Summer 1964).

15  Paul B. Sheatsley and Jacob Feldman, "National Survey on Public Reaction and Behavior," in Bradley S. Greenberg and Edwin B. Parker, eds., *The Kennedy Assassination and the American Public: Social Communication in Crisis* (Stanford, Calif.: Stanford University Press, 1965), pp. 149-77.

# PROBLEMS IN DEVELOPING INDICES
# OF NEWS VALUE*

*In reanalyzing diffusion data, the author shows that indices that ignore time of day are misleading; 'ego involvement' proves to be superior as a predictor variable.*

News value is consistently assumed to be related to the extent of diffusion of news events. However, few attempts have been made in the development of indices of news value, and no systematic effort has been made to define or clarify this concept.[1] Adjectives such as "significant," "important" and "relevant," along with phrases like "emotional appeal" and "psychological impact" have been used by various writers in an apparent reference to this variable.

This paper presents a critical discussion of two news value indices proposed in an earlier study and makes some suggestions for considering social psychological variables in the development of such indices.

Hill and Bonjean appear to be the only writers who have been interested in developing indices of news value.[2] Most studies report using a subjective criterion, or the author has simply assumed an event is unimportant or important.[3]

Hill and Bonjean suggest two indices in the form of hypotheses:

The greater the news value of an event, the more rapid will be its diffusion; and the more important interpersonal communication will be in the diffusion process.

Both appear to be based on the questionable assumption,[4] first proposed by Deutschmann and Danielson in hypothesis form,[5] that time of day does not affect the process. An examination of this assumption is in order.

*Time of Day.* Deutschmann and Danielson proposed that television plays a major role in delivering important news regardless of the time of day.[6] This hypothesis has not been supported by news diffusion studies of very unusual events, such as the assassination of the late President Kennedy,[7] and appears overdrawn even with respect to events of lesser impact.

Table 1, which reports the time of news release and percentage of audience exposed to different media for various events, does not seem to indicate consistent supremacy for TV.[8] In the morning, radio or newspapers seem to dominate as initial sources of the news. For events occurring around noon and later, TV seems to play a larger role, a tendency which apparently continues until evening, when TV tends to decline. TV is an entertainment medium and a very popular one. It is often bulletin treatment of important news that gives TV its superiority over other media as initial source of important news. Even then its supremacy is limited to certain hours,[9] as the Deutschmann and Danielson data show. First, in the Alaska story the news did not get bulletin treatment in Lansing, whereas it did in Madison.[10] Hence T.V. informed a larger proportion of the people in Madison than in Lansing.

TABLE 1
Time of News Release and Percentage of Audience Exposed to Different Media for Various Events

|  | Time of News Release | Radio | T.V. | NSP | Inter-personal |
|---|---|---|---|---|---|
| Heart Transplant[a] | 7:10 a.m. | 35 % | 12 % | 46 % | 6 % |
| Taft's Death | 7:45 a.m. | 48 | 14.6 | 10.6 | 26 |
| Eisenhower's Decision | 7:52 a.m. | 39 | 14 | 27 | 20 |
| Pope's Encyclical | 9:00 a.m. | 30.3 | 28.8 | 39.6 | 2.2 |
| Canadian Governor-General's Death[a] | 10:10 a.m. | 59 | 12.3 | 4.5 | 24.2 |
| Khrushchev's ouster | 12:00 a.m. | 34 | 35 | 12 | 19 |
| Eisenhower's Stroke | 2:30 p.m. | 32 | 38 | 12 | 18 |
| Alaskan Statehood (Lansing[b] | 6:30 p.m. | 32 | 20 | 33 | 15 |
| (Madison | 6:30 p.m. | 24 | 34 | 41 | 2 |
| Explorer I (Palo Alto | 7:30 p.m. | 18 | 61 | 10 | 10 |
| Trudeau's Marriage | 9:50 p.m. | 34 | 45 | 4 | 17 |
| Explorer I (Madison | 10:30 p.m. | 29 | 36 | 22 | 13 |
| Explorer I (Lansing | 10:30 p.m. | 20 | 40 | 17 | 23 |

[a]News released Sunday
[b]Did not receive bulletin treatment

Furthermore, Deutschmann and Danielson erred in lumping data for localities with different time-zones. As a result the Explorer I data are misleading.[11] Although Lansing and Madison were in the same time zone and hence these places received the news of Explorer I at the same time, Palo Alto is three hours behind them (10:30 p.m. vs. 7:30 P.S.T.). At the moment that most people in Lansing and Madison were getting ready to go to bed, residents of Palo Alto had just finished their dinner. Their own data from the three communities separately show (Table 1) that while in Palo Alto TV is the initial source reported by 61%, in Lansing and Madison it is 40% and 36 % respectively.

The regularity in Table 1, in spite of differences among events, is clear enough to suggest that time of day is an important variable in explaining differential exposure to TV.

*Rate of Diffusion.* Disregarding time of day produces some problems in the computation of a news value index based on the number of respondents informed of the event during a certain amount of time after the news breaks. (Hill and Bonjean suggest ranking events by percentage of respondents informed one hour after release.)[12] The difficulty arises from the fact that, when news of moderate importance is released depending on the hour, some communities get more extensive exposure from the electronic media than others. Thus the results for different time zones become incomparable. For example, Palo Alto residents, for whom the news was released at 7:30 p.m., got a longer exposure to the electronic media for the news of Explorer I than did the residents of Lansing and Madison, for whom the news was released at 10:30 p.m. Even assuming that the interpersonal channel was active only immediately after the news break, a larger proportion of the Palo Alto sample was aware of the news by "bed time" (Table 1). Thus a rate based on the percentage of respondents informed within the hour would be inflated in favor of Palo Alto.

Eisenhower's stroke occurred at 2:30 p.m. Only 26% of respondents were informed in the first hour and a half, but Explorer I, released at 10:30 p.m., shows 43% informed in the same period (Hill and Bonjean).[13] Evening is more favorable than mid-afternoon for TV exposure. Thus news value measured this way is probably inflated in favor of Explorer I.[14]

The average rate of increase in the percent of knowers hour-to-hour should yield a better measure of news value. This rate for Eisenhower story is 5.5% and for Explorer I 2.5% for every half hour. However, this method does not appear to be fool-proof either. If a story bulletined just before prime time is reported again during the prime time, exposure would show a sudden jump which would again inflate the rate.

*Interpersonal Communication.* Hill and Bonjean suggest the percentage of people who receive the news by word of mouth as another index of news value. But data comparing information from several studies, is inconsistent.[15] Although rate of diffusion is supposedly correlated with extent of interpersonal communication, in their table the news which spread more rapidly sometimes appears to have been communicated less frequently to others. For instance, in the news of Senator Taft's death, interpersonal channel accounts for 26% as source of first exposure; in the news of President Eisenhower's stroke it accounts only for

18% (Table 1).[16] In the Trudeau story, interpersonal accounts only for 17% as initial source but in the diffusion of the news of the ailing Governor-General's expected death, interpersonal accounted for 24%.[17]

Again, contrary to Deutschmann and Danielson, time of day plays some role in interpersonal communication as initial source. The news of Taft's and the Canadian Governor-General's deaths were both released in the morning, that of Eisenhower's stroke at 2:30 p.m. and Trudeau's marriage at 9:50 p.m. The interpersonal channel would have less time for activity if the news breaks close to, or at the time of, maximum exposure to electronic media (for instance, in the evening). In such a situation the potential receivers of the news by word-of-mouth would tend to be already informed.[18] Therefore, other things equal, the further the moment of the news break from the time of habitual exposure to the electronic media, the more active the interpersonal channel. This hypothesis gains indirect support from the fact that those who are at home at the time of the news-break usually hear the news before others; those who are out are more exposed to interpersonal channel.[19] The same is true of Allen and Colfax's study of the diffusion of President Johnson's unexpected announcement not to seek a second term, broadcast at 9:45 p.m., Sunday, March 31, 1968, in which the investigators discovered that only 5% of the knowers heard the news by word of mouth.[20] (However, the President's talk had been previously announced as a major policy speech, so it is not comparable to unexpected news stories such as Trudeau's secret marriage.)

After finding that rate of diffusion and amount of interpersonal communication are not reliable indices of news value, it is appropriate to explore the availability of other indices not affected by the time.

*Ego-involvement.* It has been reported that Democrats more than Republicans tended to disbelieve the assassination of President Kennedy[21] and that political opponents of the late President spent less time with radio and TV during the days following his violent death.[22] Another study found that heart specialists verified the news of the first heart transplant and engaged in discussion about it more frequently than non-specialists doctors.[23] In another study, Catholics tended to verify, tell others and be told about the news of Pope Paul's Encyclical more than the non-Catholics.[24]

One can interpret these findings in terms of stronger ego-involvement. According to Sherif and Sherif, an individual is ego-involved when one or more ego-attitudes, that is, attitudes central to one's self, participate as factors in determining his experience and behaviour.[25] It is not unreasonable to hypothesize that the more an individual is ego-involved in an event, the more he tends to check the validity of the news about that event; the more talk about it, the more he is apt

# Canadian Studies in Mass Communication

# NOTES

\* Reprinted from *Journalism Quarterly*, Vol. 50, No.3, (Autumn 1973), pp. 497-501

1. An exception is the study by Greenberg which makes a distinction between "importance" of and "attention" given a news event. See Bradley S. Greenberg, "Person to Person Communication in the Diffusion of News Events," *Journalism Quarterly*, 41:489-94 (Autumn 1964).

2. Richard J. Hill and Charles M. Bonjean, "News Diffusion: A Test of Regularity Hypothesis," *Journalism Quarterly*, 41:336-42 (Summer 1964).

3. For instance, Deutschmann and Danielson rely on what they think "an experienced newsman would say." See Paul J. Deutschmann and Wayne A. Danielson, "Diffusion of Knowledge of the Major News Story," *Journalism Quarterly*, 37:345-55 (Summer 1960). For a common sense assumption regarding the news value see, for example, Richard w. Budd, Malcolm S. MacLean Jr. and Arthur M. Barnes, "Regularities in The Diffusion of Two Major News Events,"*Journalism Quarterly*, 43:221-30 (Summer 1966); John B. Adams, James J. Mullen and Harold M. Wilson, "Diffusion of a 'Minor' Foreign Affairs News Event," *Journalism Quarterly*, 46:545-51 (Autumn 1969), and Irving L. Allen and J. David Colfax, "Diffusion of News of LBJ's March 31 Decision," *Journalism Quarterly*, 45:321-4 (Summer 1968).

4. For a criticism of the second hypothesis, see Greenberg, *op.cit.*

5. Deutschmann and Danielson, *op.cit.*

6. *Ibid.*

7. Hill and Bonjean, *op.cit.*

8 For the sources of the U.S. data in Table 1 see M. Timothy O'Keefe, "The First Heart Transplant: A Study of Diffusion Among Doctors," *Journalism Quarterly*, 46:237-42 (Summer 1969); Deutschmann and Danielson, *op. cit.*; Budd, MacLean and Barnes, *op. cit.*; Adams, Mullen and Wilson, *op.cit.*, and Hill and Bonjean, *op.cit.*. The Canadian data in Table 1 came from two studies the first about the diffusion of the news of the death of Georges Vanier, Canadian governor-general, on March 5, 1967, the second on the diffusion of news of the secret marriage of Pierre Elliott Trudeau, the 51-year-old bachelor Canadian prime minister to 22-year-old Margaret Sinclair, on March 4, 1971. Both studies were conducted by the author and are available in mimeographed from: "Diffusion of a News Event in a Canadian City" and "Diffusion of a 'Happy' News Event."

9. It is obvious that one cannot explain the supremacy of TV in the case of Eisenhower's stroke, the news of which was released around 2:30 p.m., in terms of bulletin treatment alone (See Table 1). The explanation seems to be that for events which occur in the afternoon most people are probably first exposed at news time around 5 or 6 p.m.

10. Deutschmann and Danielson, *op.cit.*

11. Deutschmann and Danielson, *ibid.*, based their interpretation of the data on the average rate for the three communities.

12. Hill and Bonjean, *op.cit.*

13. Hill and Bonjean's information about Explorer I is based on Deutschmann and Danielson's report. As already indicated, this information is inaccurate. However, as an example it serves the purpose.

14. Deutschmann and Danielson, *op.cit.*, on the basis of the percentage of respondents who talked about the news, rank the Eisenhower stroke story above the Explorer I story.

According to the indices suggested later in the present paper, this means that the Eisenhower stroke story is of greater news value.

15. Hill and Bonjean, *op.cit.*
16. For diffusion rates of Senator Taft's death and Eisenhower's stroke, see Otto N. Larsen and Richard J. Hill, "Mass Media and Interpersonal Communication in the Diffusion of a News Event," *American Sociological Review,* 19:426-33 (August, 1954), and Deutschmann and Danielson, *op. cit.*
17. Whereas it took more than 3 hours for 50% of the knowers to receive the news of Vanier's death, the same proportion came to know of Trudeau's marriage in about 15 minutes. The higher rate of interpersonal communication in the case of the Vanier story may also be attributed to the occurrence of that event on Sunday.
18. The data reported by Deutschmann and Danielson also seem to support this hypothesis. When they compare the data from Lansing and Madison on Alaskan statehood, in Lansing where the news did not get bulletin treatment 15% of the knowers received the news by word of mouth in contrast to Madison, where only 2 % received the news in this way (Table 1).
19. Hill and Bonjean, *op.cit.*
20. Allen and Colfax, *op.cit.*
21. Thomas J. Banta, "The Kennedy Assassination: Early Thoughts and Emotions," *Public Opinion Quarterly,* 28:216-24 (Summer 1964).
22. Paul B. Sheatsley and Jacob J. Feldman, "National Survey on Public Reaction and Behavior," pp. 149-77 in Bradley S. Greenberg and Edwin B. Parker, eds., *The Kennedy Assassination and the The American Public* (Stanford, California: Stanford University Press, 1965).
23. O'Keefe, *op.cit.*
24. Adams, Mullen and Wilson, *op.cit.*
25. Muzafer Sherif and Carolyn W. Sherif, *An Outline of Social Psychology* (New York: Harper and Row, 1956), pp. 582-4.
26. For example, in their paper, Budd *et al.*, although conscious of the effects of time of day when comparing an Iowa City study with a similar one in East Lansing, also disregard the time differences between the two places. Thus, if the news of Khrushchev's ouster was released at noon in Iowa City (Table 1), it must have been released at 1 p.m. in East Lansing. (The distributions of the knowers by source are 34%, 61%, 1% and 3% for radio, TV, newspaper and interpersonal respectively for East Lansing). According to the argument of the present paper, this fact makes the data for the two places noncomparable. But, Budd *et al.* attribute the difference between the two cities to the Detroit newspaper strike. See Budd, MacLean and Barnes, *op.cit.* For concern about the time of day effects see also Hill and Bonjean, *op.cit.*
27. See Greenberg, *op.cit.*; and Allen and Colfax, *op.cit.*
28. An exception is the study by Adams, Mullen and Wilson, *op.cit.*, which compares the reaction of Catholics and non-Catholics to the Pope's Encyclical.